COLONIAL WILLIAMSBURG WELCOMES YOU

*W*illiamsburg, capital of Great Britain's largest and wealthiest colony, had by 1774 become a city whose residents were part of an extraordinarily dynamic community. It was a community of patriots and Tories, of slaveholders and slaves, of dreamers and skeptics. They struggled to resolve the contradictions between their loyalties to the mother country and their families and their aspirations for freedom and independence. Some were bold enough to lead a revolution. Others were confused or angered and alienated.

Colonial Williamsburg's Revolutionary City portrays what it was like when subjects of the British monarchy turned themselves into citizens of an independent state and then fought and endured a war to achieve their freedom. Each day, the Historic Area is the site of this interactive and family-friendly program. And the themes of Revolutionary City echo across the Historic Area, asking guests to rethink their civic roles and responsibilities and encouraging greater participation in the continuing American experiment with democracy.

To visit Colonial Williamsburg's Historic Area is to see the public buildings, trade shops, and homes of the eighteenth century and to meet the people who lived and worked here. Yet it is more than that: it is also a chance to see more clearly the connections between what it took to be a good citizen in the eighteenth century and what it takes in the twenty first: courage, participation, and commitment. Now more than ever.

"That the future may learn from the past." This is the mission of Colonial Williamsburg. We strive to help our guests, and those we reach beyond this city, to draw understanding, wisdom, and inspiration from the lessons of history. Thomas Jefferson believed that an educated citizenry is the best defense of democratic freedoms. Colonial Williamsburg honors and represents, as it has for more than seventy-five years, the ideals, values, and hopes on which America was founded.

Your patronage is the single largest source of support for Colonial Williamsburg's museum and educational programs. The balance of the annual cost of preserving and maintaining the Historic Area and of presenting those programs is funded by donors' generous contributions; sales of craft objects, reproductions, and educational materials; revenues from hotel and restaurant operations; rental property income; and endowment income.

All of us at Colonial Williamsburg appreciate the many ways in which you support our programs and purposes. Your participation is essential to the long-term future of this special place.

Colin G. Campbell, *Chairman and President*
The Colonial Williamsburg Foundation

THIRD EDITION

OFFICIAL GUIDE TO COLONIAL WILLIAMSBURG

by Michael Olmert, Suzanne E. Coffman, and Paul Aron

Drawings of buildings by Peter C. Turner

Maps by Louis Luedtke

Design by Helen M. Olds and Richard Stinely

Photography by David M. Doody, Tom Green, Hans Lorenz,

Barbara Lombardi, Kelly J. Mihalcoe, and Lael White

Colonial Williamsburg

The Colonial Williamsburg Foundation

Williamsburg, Virginia

www.colonialwilliamsburg.org

Printed in the United States of America

18 17 16 15 14 13 12 11 10 09 08 07   1 2 3 4 5 6 7 8

The Library of Congress has cataloged the 1998 edition as follows:

Olmert, Michael.
    Official guide to Colonial Williamsburg / text by
Michael Olmert ; new text by Suzanne E. Coffman ;
drawings of buildings by Peter C. Turner ; maps by
Louis Luedtke. — New ed.
        p.   cm.
    Includes bibliographical references (p.   ) and index.
    ISBN 0-87935-184-5 (pbk.)
    1. Williamsburg (Va.)—Guidebooks. I. Coffman,
Suzanne E., 1958– . II. Colonial Williamsburg Foundation.
III. Title.
F234.W7046 1998
917.55'42520441—dc21   98-17476
                                                 CIP
    ISBN-13: 978-0-87935-234-9 (pbk.)
    ISBN-10: 0-87935-234-5 (pbk.)

    ISBN-13: 978-0-87935-235-6
    ISBN-10: 0-87935-235-3

Photographs taken of Colonial Williamsburg's buildings, gardens, and objects by guests must be intended for their personal use only. Such photographs may not be used for commercial purposes.

Chowning's Tavern®, Christiana Campbell's Tavern®, Colonial Williamsburg®, King's Arms Tavern®, Revolutionary City®, Shields Tavern®, WILLIAMSBURG®, WILLIAMSBURG At Home®, WILLIAMSBURG Booksellers®, WILLIAMSBURG Celebrations™, WILLIAMSBURG Collection®, WILLIAMSBURG Marketplace®, and WILLIAMSBURG Revolutions™ are marks of The Colonial Williamsburg Foundation, a not-for-profit educational institution.

The Frenchman's Map on page 16 is reproduced courtesy of Earl Gregg Swem Library, the College of William and Mary, Williamsburg, Virginia.

The detail from the portrait of Peyton Randolph on page 113 is reproduced courtesy of the Virginia Historical Society, Richmond, Virginia.

The Colonial Williamsburg Foundation
PO Box 1776
Williamsburg, VA 23187-1776
www.colonialwilliamsburg.org

CONTENTS

YOUR VISIT TO COLONIAL WILLIAMSBURG'S HISTORIC AREA

*D*ebate revolutionary ideas with Thomas Jefferson, Patrick Henry, or George Washington. See prominent colonial citizens wearing the fashions of the eighteenth century. Encounter the African-American slaves and free blacks who made the Virginia colony's prosperity possible. Watch tradespeople work in their shops. Dine in a colonial tavern on fare based on early American recipes. Experience what it was like to live in the capital of Virginia during the era of the American Revolution.

A visit to Colonial Williamsburg's Historic Area is a journey into America's past. Here, in the restored capital of eighteenth-century Virginia, you will enter the world of people who lived more than two hundred years ago. By pursuing independence, they changed the course of history. They became, instead of British subjects, American citizens.

Colonial Williamsburg's hotel properties are also among the country's premier destination resorts. Excellent dining establishments, shopping, hotels, and award-winning golf courses are all within walking distance of Colonial Williamsburg's Historic Area. Just southwest is Jamestown, where English colonization took root in 1607 and the friendship of Captain John Smith and Pocahontas grew. Just southeast is Yorktown, where George Washington and the Continental army defeated the British 174 years later. Drive about an hour southeast of Williamsburg to enjoy Virginia's beaches; drive the same distance northwest to explore the state capital and the Civil War battlefields around Richmond.

Welcome to Williamsburg.

CHECKLIST: VISITING COLONIAL WILLIAMSBURG'S HISTORIC AREA

- ☐ *Travel back in time to the era when Thomas Jefferson, Patrick Henry, and George Washington helped spark the American Revolution.*
- ☐ *Meet the patriot leaders, tradespeople, shopkeepers, laborers, and free and enslaved African Americans who created a new nation.*
- ☐ *Take in fascinating museum exhibitions, special lectures, and tours.*
- ☐ *Dine in colonial taverns and twenty-first-century restaurants.*
- ☐ *Stay in world-class hotels, tee up on award-winning golf courses, and enjoy other resort amenities just steps from the eighteenth century.*
- ☐ *Shop for Colonial Williamsburg merchandise in any of our twenty-four stores inside and adjacent to the Historic Area.*

What is Colonial Williamsburg's Historic Area? A trip to a different place and time. America's birthplace. A chance to get reacquainted with your country.

BEFORE YOU VISIT

Before you make your reservations, consider what you want to do while you're here. Review this guide to see what interests you and your family the most. For your convenience, you can now reserve hotel rooms, admission tickets, and vacation packages online.

Internet. Visit www.colonialwilliamsburg .org or www.history.org for information about the Foundation, our educational resources, the Historic Area, the calendar of events, museums, tickets, and our hotels and restaurants.

Vacation Planner. The Vacation Planner offers a general overview of Colonial Williamsburg's programs and facilities. It also contains information on the different types of admission tickets, year-round and special events, and package plans at the hotels. Call 1-800-HISTORY (447-8679) or e-mail us at cwres@cwf.org to request a copy of the Vacation Planner.

Phone-in Reservations. You can also make lodging and dining reservations and purchase

your admission and evening program tickets by calling 1-800-HISTORY (447-8679). Our guest services agents can help you select programs that will appeal to you and your family.

Why You Want to Buy a Ticket. Your admission ticket is your passport to the programs and sites in the Historic Area, our ninety acres of gardens and greens, and our world-class museums.

Talk with the patriot printer of the *Virginia Gazette*. Learn what a middle-class housewife thinks will happen to her husband and children if war comes. Find out what "all men are created equal" means to an enslaved African American. Watch master tradespeople use eighteenth-century techniques to create exquisite silver bowls, utilitarian ironwares, fashionable gowns, and functional baskets. Stand in the House of Burgesses, where Patrick Henry railed against the Stamp Act. Admire the majesty of the Governor's Palace; then learn how the "middling sort" lived at the James Geddy or Benjamin Powell House. Stroll by elegant boxwood topiaries and through informal kitchen gardens.

Continue exploring the past at our museums. See the elegant and everyday objects colonial Virginians lived with at the DeWitt Wallace Decorative Arts Museum. Admire the nation's premier collection of American folk art at the Abby Aldrich Rockefeller Folk Art Museum.

Your admission ticket does more than give you access to buildings. It opens the door to a different era.

CHECKLIST: PLANNING YOUR VISIT

To find out information or to make reservations for tickets, package plans at Colonial Williamsburg's hotels, and programs and activities during your visit

☐ *Call 1-800-HISTORY (447-8679).*

☐ *Visit Colonial Williamsburg's Web site at www.colonialwilliamsburg.org.*

Guests with Special Needs. Colonial Williamsburg wants all guests to enjoy their experience here. If you have special needs, call 1-800-246-2099 (toll-free), 1-757-220-7645 (voice), TTY 1-800-637-4677 (toll-free), or TTY 1-757-565-8620 about four weeks before your visit to schedule signing interpreters or guides for the visually impaired. More information about accessibility for guests is also available online at www.colonialwilliamsburg.org/visit/planyourvisit/accessibility.

☐ Braille guides to the Historic Area may be borrowed from Colonial Williamsburg's Visitor Center.

☐ Get information on wheelchair rentals, portable wheelchair ramps, special parking passes, parking in the Historic Area, Colonial Williamsburg's buses equipped with wheelchair lifts, and other services.

CHECKLIST: PACKING

☐ *Wear comfortable shoes. You will be walking to buildings, around them, and through them.*

☐ *Bring appropriate clothes for the weather. Summers are hot and humid. Spring and fall days can change quickly from temperate to warm or cold. The usually mild winters can be punctuated by days in the single digits. Check the long-range forecast before you visit.*

☐ *Include jacket and tie if you will be having dinner in the Regency Room at the Williamsburg Inn (jacket only for Sunday brunch). Casual dress is appropriate everywhere else.*

Because of limited accessibility at some sites, guests with disabilities receive a discount on admission tickets. The Visitor Center,

Your admission ticket is your passport to the sites and programs in the Historic Area.

CHECKLIST: GETTING TO WILLIAMSBURG

☐ *By car: Williamsburg is located 150 miles south of Washington, D.C., midway between Richmond and Norfolk. Take Interstate 64 to exit 238. After exiting, follow Route 143 east for a half mile. Turn right onto Route 132. Go about a mile and a half. Turn left onto Route 132Y (Visitor Center Drive). Colonial Williamsburg's Visitor Center is on your left.*

☐ *By air: Newport News/Williamsburg*

International Airport is twenty minutes from Williamsburg; Richmond International Airport and Norfolk International Airport are fifty minutes away. All have rental car and limousine services.

☐ *By train or bus: Amtrak serves the Williamsburg Transportation Center with a connecting train from Washington, D.C. The center is just blocks from the Historic Area and provides car rentals, a cab stand, and Greyhound bus connections.*

hotels, and twenty-first-century restaurants, shops, and museums are largely accessible.

International Guests. At the Visitor Center, international guests can listen to French, German, Italian, Japanese, Portuguese, Russian, or Spanish while viewing the film *Williamsburg—The Story of a Patriot*. Brochures in French, German, Japanese, Spanish, and Chinese are also available at the Visitor Center.

How Long to Visit. Plan to stay several days. It's next to impossible to do everything there is to do in Colonial Williamsburg's Historic Area in a single day. Make your reservations as early as possible, especially for Easter, Thanksgiving, and the Christmas season. Then travel across the miles to Williamsburg, where you'll travel back in time to the era of the American Revolution.

AFTER YOU ARRIVE

At the Visitor Center. You can buy your tickets at several Colonial Williamsburg ticketing locations and at many local hotels and motels, but all guests should begin their trip into the past at the Visitor Center. If you have not already purchased your tickets and made lodging, dining, and evening program reservations, the Visitor Center staff can help you plan your visit, select the appropriate ticket options, and make reservations for dining, lodging, and special programs. You may also want to stop by the Learning Resource Center at the Visitor Center to learn about programs that appeal to children. (See the Educational Services section on page 172 for more information on the Learning Resource Center.) With your ticket you will receive a copy of the weekly program guide, which lists the programs being offered in the Historic Area and the museums. Be sure to see *Williamsburg—The Story of a Patriot.* This dramatization of events in Williamsburg on the eve of the American Revolution plays throughout the day at the Visitor Center and in most area hotel and motel rooms.

Other Ticket Sales Locations. Tickets and information are also available at the Lumber House ticket office and Tickets, Treasures, and Books, both in the Historic Area, and the Merchants Square Ticket Office, which is adjacent to the Historic Area. Guests of Colonial Williamsburg's hotels can also purchase tickets at the Williamsburg Inn and the Williamsburg Lodge. Several Williamsburg-area hotels and motels also offer Colonial Williamsburg admission tickets, although they do not have evening or special program tickets.

Orientation Walk, Walking Tours, Carriage and Wagon Rides. When available, the thirty-minute orientation walks provide a quick overview of the town and the things you can see and do in the Historic Area. Sixty-minute walking tours, offered mid-March through December, explore topics such as the American Revolution, African-American life in colonial Virginia, religion in the colony, and consumerism during the eighteenth century. Make reservations for walking tours at any ticket sales location on the day of the walk. Tickets for carriage or wagon rides

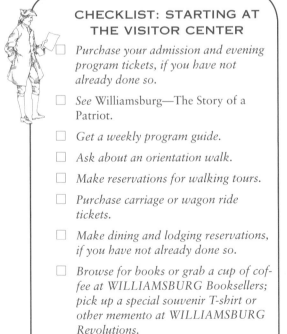

CHECKLIST: STARTING AT THE VISITOR CENTER

☐ *Purchase your admission and evening program tickets, if you have not already done so.*

☐ *See* Williamsburg—The Story of a Patriot.

☐ *Get a weekly program guide.*

☐ *Ask about an orientation walk.*

☐ *Make reservations for walking tours.*

☐ *Purchase carriage or wagon ride tickets.*

☐ *Make dining and lodging reservations, if you have not already done so.*

☐ *Browse for books or grab a cup of coffee at* WILLIAMSBURG *Booksellers; pick up a special souvenir T-shirt or other memento at* WILLIAMSBURG *Revolutions.*

☐ *Take the bus or walk the Bridge to the Past to the Historic Area.*

can be purchased at any ticket sales location on the day of the ride. Rides sell out quickly during peak seasons, so buy your tickets early in the day.

Colonial Williamsburg Buses. As you leave the Visitor Center, you will find buses waiting to take you directly to the Historic Area. All guests of Colonial Williamsburg's hotels and all guests who have purchased admission tickets may ride our shuttle buses. Streets in the Historic Area are closed to motor vehicles, and there is no regular guest parking there. If you are staying at one of Colonial Williamsburg's hotels, leave your car at your hotel and walk or take the bus to the Historic Area. If you are staying somewhere else, leave your car at the Visitor Center and walk or take the bus from there.

The Bridge to the Past. The five-hundred-foot pedestrian bridge connects Colonial Williamsburg's Visitor Center with a path that reaches the Historic Area. Plaques embedded in the walkway help prepare guests for their transitions to and from the eighteenth century.

CHECKLIST:
FOR THE FIRST-TIME GUEST

☐ *Governor's Palace (allow an hour). The residence of seven royal governors and the first two elected governors of Virginia, the Palace is shown today as the home of Lord Dunmore, the British governor on the eve of the Revolution.*

☐ *Peyton Randolph House (allow 45 minutes). The home of one of Virginia's leading politicians. In the backyard, see the work undertaken by enslaved men and women.*

☐ *Courthouse (allow 20 minutes). Participate in a wide variety of court trials in which lives, liberties, and property come into contest.*

☐ *Magazine (allow 30 minutes). The warehouse for gunpowder and firearms belonging to the colony and then the Commonwealth of Virginia.*

☐ *Printing Office and Bookbindery (allow 20 minutes). Newspapers, political notices, and other printed items played a key role before and during the Revolution.*

☐ *James Anderson Blacksmith Shop (allow 30 minutes). During the Revolution, Anderson and his men repaired arms for the American forces.*

☐ *Capitol (allow 40 minutes). Here Virginia's patriots voted for independence and a new state constitution.*

☐ *The Museums of Colonial Williamsburg (allow at least an hour). The DeWitt Wallace Decorative Arts Museum features world-class English and American silver, ceramics, paintings, prints, and textiles dating from 1600 to 1830. The Abby Aldrich Rockefeller Folk Art Museum is the first museum dedicated solely to American folk art.*

☐ *Revolutionary City (allow up to two hours). A series of dramatic scenes about the lives of Virginians before and during the American Revolution played out on the streets of Williamsburg.*

All sites recommended above require an admission ticket. Visit a ticket sales location or consult the weekly program guide for ticketing options and for daily schedules.

SIGNIFICANT MOMENTS IN WILLIAMSBURG'S HISTORY

1607 First permanent English settlement in North America established at Jamestown.

1693 Charter granted for the College of William and Mary.

1699 Virginia's capital moves from Jamestown to Williamsburg.

1765 *May 30.* Patrick Henry delivers his ringing Caesar-Brutus speech in opposition to the Stamp Act.

1769 Virginia protests new British taxes and boycotts British goods.

1774 *June 1.* Williamsburg citizens observe a day of fasting, humiliation, and prayer to protest Parliament's closing of the port of Boston.

August. Virginia's leaders elect delegates to the first Continental Congress in Philadelphia.

1775 *April 21.* Virginia royal governor Lord Dunmore has the colony's powder removed from the Magazine. Only the efforts of Williamsburg's moderate leaders prevent an angry mob from marching on the Governor's Palace.

June 8. The royal governor and his family flee the Palace.

November 15. Dunmore issues a proclamation offering freedom to slaves willing to fight for the British.

1776 *May 15.* Virginia's legislators instruct their delegates in Philadelphia to propose independence, leading directly to the adoption of the Declaration of Independence on July 4.

June 12. Virginia adopts America's first Declaration of Rights, later the basis for the Bill of Rights of the U.S. Constitution.

July 6. Patrick Henry inaugurated first governor of the state of Virginia.

1780 Capital moves from Williamsburg to Richmond.

1781 *June 25–July 4.* British occupy Williamsburg.

September 14. Washington and Rochambeau arrive in Williamsburg to plan campaign against British at Yorktown.

October 19. British surrender at Yorktown, effectively ending the Revolution.

1862 *May 5.* Battle of Williamsburg. Union forces occupy Williamsburg for the rest of the Civil War.

1926 John D. Rockefeller Jr. decides to restore Williamsburg to its eighteenth-century appearance.

1934 President Franklin D. Roosevelt commemorates the restoration, referring to Duke of Gloucester Street as "the most historic avenue in America."

1999 The City of Williamsburg celebrates its three hundredth anniversary.

THE CITY OF WILLIAMSBURG

"WILLIAMSBURG . . . is regularly laid out in parallel streets, intersected by others at right angles; has a handsome square in the center, through which runs the principal street, one of the most spacious in North-America, three quarters of a mile in length, and above a hundred feet wide. At the ends of this street are two public buildings, the college and the capitol: and although the houses are of wood, covered with shingles, and but indifferently built, the whole makes a handsome appearance."

—The Reverend Andrew Burnaby, who came to Virginia from England in 1759 and remained until 1760, described Williamsburg in his *Travels through the Middle Settlements in North-America, in the Years 1759 and 1760*

JAMESTOWN, THE SEVENTEENTH-CENTURY CAPITAL

The story of Williamsburg, the capital of eighteenth-century Virginia, really began at seventeenth-century Jamestown. For over ninety years after the first English adventurers set foot on Virginia soil, Jamestown served as the seat of government and administrative center of England's largest colony in North America. From its statehouse on the banks of the James River, officials and lawmakers governed the colonists, promoted the spread of settlement, and, tragically for the future, displaced Indians from their native lands and sanctioned the importation of African slaves for their labor.

When the statehouse burned for the fourth time in 1698, many Virginians, including the royal governor, Francis Nicholson, seized on the accident as an opportunity to move the capital. Several prospective sites were considered. After some debate, members of the House of Burgesses chose a propitious site between the York and James Rivers five miles from the old capital city, an up-and-coming place known as Middle Plantation.

Middle Plantation had been founded in the early seventeenth century as an outpost to defend against Indian attacks. By 1690, it had developed into a prosperous neighborhood of widely scattered houses belonging to successful tobacco planters and merchants. It also contained a church, several stores, a tavern, two mills, and, after 1695, the first building of the College of William and Mary. On several occasions, most notably during Bacon's Rebellion in 1676 and 1677, when Jamestown was burned to the ground, Middle Plantation served as a substitute capital. Its main attractions as a potential site for the capital were several. First, it was located on high ground between two rivers and therefore was relatively healthy. Its inland location was thought to be safe from naval bombardment, and it was already the home of the college, one of Virginia's principal institutions. Finally, and perhaps most important, several of Virginia's leading politicians lived in Middle Plantation. Begun in 1699, the new city was named Williamsburg in honor of the king of England, William III.

The Frenchman's Map, probably drawn by a French officer for the purpose of billeting troops after the Siege of Yorktown in 1781, shows the streets and many of the buildings of eighteenth-century Williamsburg.

WILLIAMSBURG'S TOWN PLAN AND LANDMARKS

Once the decision was made to move the capital from Jamestown to Middle Plantation, an entirely new capital city was laid out on the site. The desire to design a completely new city fulfilled one of the reasons for moving the capital from Jamestown. Many Virginians thought their colony was becoming too important to be served by anything less than a capital city built to reflect Virginia's preeminence among England's American colonies. In all probability, Governor Nicholson took the initiative for the new design. He had successfully planned Annapolis as governor of Maryland, and he was well versed in the latest principles of urban planning. The town plan of Williamsburg reflected those principles. The fact that it was newly built can be your key to discovering in restored Williamsburg

traces of the eighteenth-century city. Several important physical landmarks were central to Nicholson's plan and are still extant.

The first is a large, open area in the center of the town known as Market Square. Today you will find the Magazine, built on Governor Alexander Spotswood's orders in 1715, and the Courthouse on Market Square. In the eighteenth century, the square served as a town common where markets and fairs were held regularly. Another distinctive feature of the colonial capital that is still present today crosses the square in an east-west direction. Duke of Gloucester Street, or "the Main Street," as it was known in the eighteenth century, extends "uptown" from the College of William and Mary at the western end and "downtown" to the Capitol building at the eastern. Ninety-nine feet wide and nearly one mile long, this street was a broad, open avenue that highlighted the linear aspects of the city plan.

To the west of Market Square, the city was laid out in the shape of a square centered on Bruton Parish Church. The first church building, completed by 1683, stood a little to the north of the present structure, which replaced it in 1715. Farther to the west is the main college building, called the Wren Building in honor of Sir Christopher Wren, an important seventeenth-century English architect who was reputed (mistakenly) to have inspired its design. Located just outside the eighteenth-century city boundary, the college building was the key visual element at the west end of Duke of Gloucester Street. The symbolic importance of this part of Williamsburg with its religious and educational institutions was and still is reinforced by the Governor's Palace. By its location at the head of a wide, green avenue running north from the church, this landmark was meant to command an eighteenth-century visitor's attention, as it still does that of modern guests.

If you walk east from Market Square, you will be drawn to the dominant landmark designed for that end of town—the Capitol. To help focus attention on this most important building, the eastern end of Williamsburg was framed by two back streets, Nicholson on the north and Francis on the south.

THE NEW TOWNS OF THE EIGHTEENTH CENTURY

People's early expectations for Williamsburg were inspired by an older vision of what cities could accomplish. Traditionally they were viewed as centers of learning, religion, and government. As you walk along Williamsburg's main street, you can see that the city planners anchored the town on the college, church, and Capitol, the physical symbols of a traditional city. An eighteenth-century visitor to Williamsburg, when it was still little more than a grid of vacant lots,

would have known from these three official buildings that he was in a capital city. But even as Williamsburg began to grow, this older understanding of what a city was meant to be was being supplanted by a newer vision.

In England, in her overseas colonies, and throughout western Europe, people who once were content to acquire relatively few material possessions began to demand more—more clothes, more crockery, more furniture, more books. This surge in consumer demand transformed villages and towns into something that not even great metropolitan cities such as London had been before. Some grew into manufacturing centers, making the goods that consumers increasingly began to demand. Others became retail centers selling affordable goods to regional markets of ordinary buyers.

The effect of this shift toward commerce-centered urban activities was even felt in far-off Virginia. By the mid-eighteenth century, Williamsburg had taken on a more modern look. Retail stores lined the streets, their display windows filled with merchandise priced to suit almost every man's and woman's pocketbook. Artisans such as silversmiths and blacksmiths frequently sold imported goods in their shops. Amid the business of government,

The Bodleian Plate, an engraved copperplate of about 1740, was discovered at Oxford University. The top row shows the College of William and Mary. The middle row has renderings of the Capitol and the Governor's Palace, which assisted in the reconstruction of those buildings.

Williamsburg catered to a growing number of eager new consumers. Because there is much that you will recognize of our own world here, restored Williamsburg is a bridge to that time when the consumer age was just beginning.

THE WILLIAMSBURG COMMUNITY

Unlike Jamestown, Williamsburg did not remain an undeveloped administrative center. Partly because the colony's growth continued throughout the eighteenth century and partly because economic forces reshaped Virginia society, Williamsburg fulfilled the expectation of its founders and kept pace with the growing colony.

At first the business of government attracted the nucleus of Williamsburg's urban population. Joining the small staff already living at the college were the governor, his household, and the clerks of various government offices. Soon the regular meetings of the General Court, the attendance of councillors on the governor, and the periodic meetings of the General Assembly brought a number of other people to Williamsburg to support these governmental activities. Taverns were established to feed and house those in town on government business. Lawyers settled here

to be close to the General Court. As the century progressed, more and more stores were opened to provide merchandise to residents and out-of-town shoppers. The townspeople engaged in these activities needed to be housed and provided with foodstuffs that they didn't grow themselves. Carpenters and masons moved to town to build houses and shops. Bakers, tailors, and barbers settled here to serve both visitors and townspeople. Much of the heavy and domestic work around town was performed by blacks, most of them enslaved, although a few were free. By the eve of the American Revolution nearly two thousand men, women, and children—roughly half white, half black—lived in the capital city.

Together these men and women formed a complex community that left traces that you can still see if you pay close attention. As you walk toward the Capitol from Market Square, for example, the increasing density of artisans' shops, stores, taverns, and houses crowding in on the Capitol gives the correct impression that this was the busiest section of town. The townspeople who lived and worked here competed for the business of visitors to the Capitol. A different landscape can be seen around the Courthouse. As you look north and south,

The Magazine was erected in 1715. After the Revolution, it saw use as a market, a Baptist meetinghouse, a dancing school, and a livery stable.

The Prentis Store is Williamsburg's best surviving example of a colonial store. Built in 1739–1740, it survived into the twentieth century as an automobile service station.

several large town houses meet the eye, as they would have in the late eighteenth century. The clamor of marketplace vendors notwithstanding, the open space of Market Square had a special appeal for the prominent men who built these imposing dwellings; it provided an attractive setting for their homes. After mid-century, the long, open avenue in front of the Governor's Palace offered a similar attraction. Earlier it had faced a jumble of small houses, noisy, dirty workshops, and a theater. Even after the large houses came to be built, the working character of Palace Green lingered here and there.

As you walk past Bruton Parish Church toward the college, you can still glimpse several small, open fields that gave something of a pastoral air to the west end of Williamsburg in the eighteenth century. A few stores, artisans' shops, and taverns line the streets here, but from a businessman's point of view this end of town was not as desirable as downtown near the Capitol. It was common for townspeople living here to buy half-acre lots in blocks of two or more, which they turned into small urban estates. Kitchen and flower gardens filled much of the open space and reinforced the residential character that Nicholson intended for this part of the capital. The back streets of Williamsburg—Prince George, Scotland, Ireland, and especially Francis and Nicholson Streets as they extended to the east—strengthened this countrified aspect of the town. Gentry houses, which amounted to large urban estates, were situated along the north and south boundaries of the town. In the eighteenth century, the distinction between town and country was blurred.

Eighteenth-century travelers to Williamsburg would have experienced some of the same sensations that the restored city offers modern guests, and others that were utterly different. They would have encountered the hustle and bustle of shops, taverns, and stores. They would have savored pleasing vistas and hurried past byways. They would have heard the sounds of people working, the ringing of bells at the college, church, and Capitol, and the rattle of carriages and wagons moving along the streets. On the way out of town travelers might have held their noses when passing the bodies of criminals left on the gibbet or stood aside to allow passage of a string of slaves in chains on the road from

Yorktown to the auction block in the busy capital. Williamsburg in the eighteenth century was a wide-open American town—alive and vibrant—on the edge of empire. You are invited to conjure up the colonial capital in your imagination as you tour the city today.

The restored buildings, antique furnishings, and costumed interpreters can help you re-create a picture of the past in your mind's eye. The townspeople themselves are always the hardest to envision and understand. There are clues everywhere. Look at how people dress and listen to how they speak. Colonial towns and cities attracted concentrations of immigrants not to be found in the countryside. Newcomers with skills in the fashion trades found ready employment in commercial centers such as Williamsburg. Town dwellers were eager to engage the services of foreign-trained tutors, dancing masters, doctors, and clerks.

The capital city was seldom the final destination for slaves fresh off the boat from Africa or the West Indies. Usually they were sold directly to planters who broke them in by working them as field hands. Williamsburg's sizable black population was largely native born. Those African Virginians who lived and worked in Williamsburg had often learned trades, could read, cipher, and sometimes write, usually spoke English, and generally were familiar with the ways of white people, however much they kept their own customs among themselves. Interpreters in Colonial Williamsburg's Historic Area can show you all aspects of the urban slave's experience.

Native Americans were seen on these streets, too. Local Indian groups had long since been reduced in number and confined to settlements on land that nobody else wanted. But now and then, local Indians found their way into town. Archaeologists excavate pottery that suggests Native Americans made and traded earthenware bowls and pots used in kitchens and quarters. Occasionally, ambassadors from the Cherokee, Nottoway, and Catawba nations led delegations to the colonial capital to treat with the governor and his Council.

Williamsburg was a place to which many came seeking their fortunes, however meager they may have been for slaves, Indians, and immigrants with few skills. The town was a crucible where people from different backgrounds shaped and were shaped by their encounters with one another. The ceaseless tug-of-war among the diverse peoples who met in North America and settled in towns like Williamsburg receives special attention today from Colonial Williamsburg's interpreters

The John Crump House before and after reconstruction.

". . . we mutually pledge to each other our Lives, our Fortunes, and our sacred Honor."

In the crucial decade before the American Revolution, Williamsburg was a training ground for a remarkable body of men. When it became clear that war with Great Britain could not be avoided, George Wythe, Richard Henry Lee, Thomas Jefferson, Benjamin Harrison, Thomas Nelson, Francis Lightfoot Lee, and Carter Braxton met in Philadelphia with representatives from the other colonies to declare independence from the mother country. On July 4, 1776, the Continental Congress formally adopted the Declaration of Independence and took the first momentous step toward establishing a new nation.

George Wythe
Richard Henry Lee
Th Jefferson
Benj Harrison
Thos Nelson jr.
Francis Lightfoot Lee
Carter Braxton

G Washington

George Washington did not sign the Declaration of Independence because in July 1776 he was in New York preparing to defend Manhattan against the British.

because those encounters forged our American values and eventually our very identity. The struggle to be both free and equal has been a dynamic force in our democracy for more than two hundred years.

WILLIAMSBURG AND THE REVOLUTION

Anyone looking up, on May 15, 1776, at the cupola on Williamsburg's Capitol would have seen an extraordinary sight. The Union Jack was gone, replaced by the red and white stripes of the "Union Flag of the American states." Virginia had declared itself "for Independency."

America's founding generation had turned the world upside down. They had thrown off the chains of monarchy and created a government in which the people were sovereign. They had turned Americans from subjects to citizens. This great experiment—democracy—continues today.

During the decades before the Revolution, the House of Burgesses, the elected lower house of the Virginia General Assembly that met in Williamsburg, had consolidated its political influence at the expense of the royal governor and his Council. Within the House of Burgesses, some of Virginia's leaders protested imperial policies and began to articulate a distinctly American political philosophy. Long before talk of independence, Patrick Henry, as a newly elected burgess in May 1765, introduced strongly worded resolutions against the despised Stamp Act and delivered his famous Caesar-Brutus speech. Long experience in local and provincial government strengthened many Virginians' resolve as the challenge to British rule gained momentum.

In May 1774, the burgesses resolved that June 1—the day the British would close Boston's harbor in retaliation for the Boston Tea Party—would be observed, in a show of unity with their fellow colonists, as a day of fasting, humiliation, and prayer in Virginia. Lord Dunmore, the royal governor, responded by dissolving the Assembly. Eighty-nine burgesses then met at the Raleigh Tavern, where they issued one of the first appeals for a continental congress. In August, the first Virginia Convention met in Williamsburg and named Virginia delegates to the Congress in Philadelphia. One of those delegates, Peyton Randolph, would be elected president of the first Continental Congress.

In March 1775, the second Virginia Convention accepted a committee report calling for a volunteer company of cavalry or infantry for defense in every county. In April, just days after minutemen and militia engaged British troops at Lexington and Concord, British mariners, following Dunmore's orders, sneaked into the Magazine in Williamsburg in the early morning hours and took fifteen half-barrels of powder. Patriots threatened to retaliate, but Randolph, Virginia's most influential political leader, negotiated a truce.

Peace would not last much longer.

In early June, Dunmore called the General Assembly into session to consider a British peace offer, but, after a second incident at the Magazine during which three local boys were injured, the governor and his family fled the Palace and never returned. In August, King George III proclaimed the colonies to be in a state of rebellion. In November, from a ship off the Virginia coast, Dunmore issued a proclamation declaring martial law and freeing slaves of rebels (patriots) willing to join the British forces.

In May 1776, Virginia became the first colony to direct its delegates in the Congress to introduce a motion for independence, and, the following month, the fifth Virginia Convention adopted America's first declaration of rights. Drafted mainly by George Mason, it heralded a new era in which written statements of individual liberties became a hallmark of American constitutional thinking. Later that month, the Convention adopted the new state constitution and chose Patrick Henry as the first governor of the independent Commonwealth of Virginia. In July, Henry officially proclaimed the Declaration of Independence.

The war years took their toll on the citizens of Williamsburg. In 1780, for reasons similar to those offered in 1699—military defense, healthier climate, and a more central location—proponents of a new capital prevailed. The capital of Revolutionary Virginia moved to Richmond, where it remains today. In April 1781, the American traitor–turned–British general Benedict Arnold under the command of Major General William Phillips seized Williamsburg and raised the British flag once again over the Capitol, and, in June, the British general Lord Cornwallis established his headquarters at the President's House at the College of William and Mary. In July, Cornwallis and his troops evacuated the town. In September, George Washington and his troops arrived in Williamsburg.

From there, it was only a few miles and a few weeks to the decisive victory of the American and French troops at Yorktown.

REVOLUTIONARY CITY

On the streets of Williamsburg today, you can join the American Revolution. Colonial Williamsburg's Historic Area is the setting for Revolutionary City, a series of interactive street performances in which actor-interpreters portray events that led to American independence.

The performances are played out over three days. "Collapse of the Royal Government" covers the period between May 1774 and May 1776 as Revolutionary ideas divide loyalties, even within families. Lord Dunmore dissolves the House of Burgesses. Arianna Randolph, a loyalist, warns her daughter Susannah that her father's loyalty to the British king may force them to leave for England. A court of tar and feathers awaits any who challenge the patriots' cause. Enslaved people gather to consider Dunmore's offer of freedom to those who take up arms against their rebel masters. Carpenter Alexander Hoy and his wife, Barbry, engage in a public argument about his enlisting. And representatives of the free men of Virginia pass resolutions for independence.

"Citizens at War" follows the triumphs and travails the residents of war-torn Williamsburg faced between June 1776 and September 1781. The Declaration of Independence is read to the citizens of Williamsburg. A merchant draws a crowd of angry protesters upset about the high prices of goods and the collapse of Virginia's currency. Barbry Hoy reappears to tell grim stories of her husband's capture and American defeats in South Carolina. British general Benedict Arnold, the American turncoat, seizes Williamsburg with Crown forces and raises the British flag over the Capitol. An African-American preacher talks about his hopes for a society where all citizens are equal. Later, General Washington addresses his men and the citizens of Williamsburg as he prepares to leave for Yorktown.

"Nation Builders," a third day of Revolutionary City programming, explores the lives of America's founders—not just the famous but also little-known men and women who quietly built a new nation as they went about their daily lives. Founders reflect on the future of the new Republic. Martha Washington visits the war-torn capital, and enslaved people consider their plight in light of the Declaration of Independence.

The program continues after dark. A capital ball features music, dance, and revelry celebrating the arrival of Lady Dunmore amid a backdrop of political intrigue. In another evening scene, Dunmore's gunpowder plot, which left the colony defenseless, is revealed to angry townspeople.

Throughout the Historic Area, you'll hear more about the trials of townspeople experiencing a town in crisis. As a guest of Colonial Williamsburg, you'll be a participant in these world-changing events. Like the citizens of Williamsburg, you may be asked: "How say ye?"

WILLIAMSBURG AFTER THE WAR

Despite the loss of the capital, Williamsburg did not die as Jamestown had. It continued to be a county seat, and it continued to house two important institutions—the College of William and Mary and the Public Hospital for the insane. Throughout the nineteenth century, Williamsburg served as a major market center for nearby farmers and their families. As a quiet college and market town, it witnessed the Civil War firsthand, experienced the emancipation of slaves, and welcomed the railroad in the 1880s. Although fires occasionally raged in parts of the old city, Williamsburg was spared major destruction. Old eighteenth-century homes were repaired, renovated, and continued in use until the twentieth century.

Then, in the early years of the twentieth century, the Reverend W. A. R. Goodwin, rector of Bruton Parish Church, had a visionary idea. Inspired by the surviving eighteenth-century character of Williamsburg and its pre-eminent role during the American Revolution, he dreamed of restoring Virginia's colonial capital to its former glory.

Goodwin felt that historic sites such as Williamsburg were national treasures to be preserved. They would not only introduce future generations to colonial history but also stand as reminders of the stirring events, principles, and people that fostered the birth of a new nation. Goodwin said, "The best way to look at history is through windows. There are windows here, and there were others, which might be restored, through which unparalleled vistas open into the nation's past."

Goodwin's efforts to enlist support for his vision initially met with little success. Then, in 1926, he persuaded John D. Rockefeller Jr., heir to the Standard Oil fortune, to tour Williamsburg. Challenged by the opportunity to restore an entire colonial community, Rockefeller agreed to support and fund the project on one condition—that it would encompass the entire town, not just parts of it.

His enthusiastic commitment continued for thirty years.

The renaissance of the colonial capital began with the purchase of the Ludwell-Paradise House in 1926. Then the real work began. It was a massive undertaking because Rockefeller and Goodwin planned more than the mere preservation of historic buildings and settings. They intended to re-create and interpret colonial life as well.

Extensive research was undertaken to ensure historical accuracy throughout the project. Research focused on period maps, deeds, inventories, plans, contemporary drawings, and accounts of the colonial capital. Early photographs documenting the exterior appearances of many of the historic buildings enhanced the restoration efforts.

Perhaps the most important find, however, was an engraved copperplate discovered in the Bodleian Library at Oxford University in England. It was the only known eighteenth-century architectural drawing of the colonial capital's principal buildings, and it became the basis for the restoration and reconstruction of those structures. In fact, Rockefeller called the Bodleian Plate the "foundation upon which we have based the restoration of the Wren Building and the reconstruction of the Governor's Palace and the Capitol. Without it, we would be acting in the dark; with it, we have gone forward with absolute certainty and conviction." The engraved copperplate is on display in the Bassett Hall Reception Building.

Meanwhile, archaeological research revealed much about eighteenth-century life. Exploratory cross-trenching unearthed the remains of the Governor's Palace in 1930, including foundation walls, steps, doorways, stone passageways, and the cellar. Additional artifacts discovered there offered guidance for faithfully reconstructing paneling, the hall's black-and-white marble floor, and other features. Archaeologists also recovered fragments of brick, stone steps, fireplace tiles, hinges,

Dr. W. A. R. Goodwin (left), *who dreamed of restoring eighteenth-century Williamsburg, and John D. Rockefeller Jr., who made the dream a reality.*

shutter fasteners, locks, and keys. These discoveries and the Bodleian Plate guided the reconstruction of the Governor's Palace on its original eighteenth-century foundations.

Gradually, many aspects of colonial life came into focus. Research revealed not only the painstaking craftsmanship of colonial designers and builders but also a new, uniquely American adaptation of classical architectural traditions. In addition, there were insights into the vibrant cultures, lifestyles, and thoughts of colonial residents. They reflected the Age of Enlightenment as well as the Revolutionary concepts of self-expression, self-determination, and individualism that ultimately led to the birth of a vital new nation with a character all its own.

Colonial Williamsburg now operates the world's largest living history museum. The thriving Historic Area, with its knowledgeable costumed interpreters, offers an opportunity to step back in time and experience a taste of eighteenth-century life. The work begun by the Reverend W. A. R. Goodwin and John D. Rockefeller Jr. continues today. An endowment established by Rockefeller supports ongoing research and educational programs in the restored colonial capital.

Colonial Williamsburg's Historic Area is a tribute to the far-sighted, dedicated efforts of the Reverend Dr. Goodwin and John D. Rockefeller Jr. and to the people whose lives they commemorated, the inhabitants of eighteenth-century Williamsburg. Rockefeller himself best described the mammoth restoration effort: "As the work has progressed, I have come to feel that perhaps an even greater value is the lesson that it teaches of the patriotism, high purpose, and unselfish devotion of our forefathers to the common good."

As you walk through historic Williamsburg, remember that it is not just a living museum but a living city as well. Many of the restored and reconstructed homes and outbuildings are residences for Colonial Williamsburg's employees; others are hotel facilities. The Historic Area is also the heart of a modern city of approximately twelve thousand residents, which in turn serves a metropolitan area of more than one hundred thousand people. Colonial Williamsburg's Historic Area, museums, and retail shops are operated by the Colonial Williamsburg Foundation, a not-for-profit educational organization. The city is administered by a mayor, council, and city manager.

GOVERNOR'S
INN

LAFAYETTE

5

Governor's
Palace

Gateway
Building

4

Peyton
Randolph
House

7

Bruton Parish
Church

NICHOLSON   STREET

1

DUKE   OF   GLOUCESTER   STREET

6

Magazine

2

Wren Building

FRANCIS   STREET

8

Public Hospital

WILLIAMSBURG
INN

WILLIAMSBURG
LODGE

LOOKING
NORTH

RICHMOND ROAD

JAMESTOWN ROAD

VISITING THE HISTORIC AREA

There is no right or wrong way to visit the Historic Area. Whether you start at the Capitol, the Governor's Palace, or the Shoemaker's Shop, you will find plenty to see and do. Tour every site or concentrate on just a few.

Some sites and activities are centered in and around the Capitol, Governor's Palace, and Peyton Randolph House. Others are scattered throughout the Historic Area. The following is a brief description of what you will find in the restored town. For more information,

The Historic Area is divided into the following eight geographical areas:

The following buildings serve as orientation landmarks:

MAGAZINE

CAPITOL

RALEIGH TAVERN

BRUTON PARISH CHURCH

GOVERNOR'S PALACE

PUBLIC HOSPITAL

PEYTON RANDOLPH HOUSE

WREN BUILDING

see the Street by Street section of this guide. The section numbers correspond to the areas identified on the above map.

Check your weekly program guide, which you will receive with your admission ticket, to find out which sites are open and which activities are being offered on the day of your visit. The program guide also lists times and locations.

If you would like more of an orientation before you start your visit, stop first at the Gateway building (open seasonally), across from Robertson's Windmill. The Gateway is conveniently located at the end of the walking path from the Visitor Center, just as you enter the Historic Area. If you take the bus from the Visitor Center, the Gateway is at your first stop. Also available at the building are sundry items to help make your visit comfortable and enjoyable.

CHECKLIST: DINING AND SHOPPING IN THE HISTORIC AREA

SECTION OF THE HISTORIC AREA	DINING	SHOPPING
1. MARKET SQUARE Near the Courthouse and Magazine	Chowning's Tavern	Market Square stands (open seasonally)
2. FROM MARKET SQUARE TO THE CAPITOL Near the Printing Office and Bookbindery		M. Dubois Grocer Post Office Prentis Store
Near the Raleigh Tavern	King's Arms Tavern Shields Tavern	The Golden Ball Raleigh Tavern Bakery Tarpley's Store
3. THE CAPITOL AND ITS SURROUNDINGS Near the Capitol	Christiana Campbell's Tavern	Tickets, Treasures, and Books
4–5. AROUND PALACE GREEN AND THE GOVERNOR'S PALACE Near the Governor's Palace		McKenzie Shop
6. FROM PALACE GREEN TO THE COLLEGE OF WILLIAM AND MARY Near Bruton Parish Church		Colonial Nursery (open seasonally) John Greenhow Store Mary Dickinson Store

A blue box indicates that you need an admission ticket to see an attraction.

SECTION 1
MARKET SQUARE

■**Courthouse.** Learn how the colonial legal system regulated and affected the lives of ordinary citizens. During presentations of "Order in the Court!" you may become the defendant, a witness, or one of the justices in a reenactment of a real trial from the eighteenth century.

■**Magazine** and **Guardhouse.** The Magazine served as the arsenal for the Virginia colony. See the authentic firearms and military equipment displayed here and listen as armorers and guards tell the story of British and American military forces in Virginia from the French and Indian War to the War for American Independence.

A replica of a 1750 Newsham patent fire engine is housed in a lean-to on the west wall of the Guardhouse.

SECTION 2
FROM MARKET SQUARE
TO THE CAPITOL

■**The Golden Ball** (Silversmith). Several silversmiths worked in eighteenth-century Williamsburg. Today at the shop of James Craig, you can watch skilled artisans use the tools and methods of their predecessors to create beautiful sterling silver flatware and hollowware.

■**James Anderson Blacksmith Shop.** At the peak of operation, blacksmith James Anderson employed around forty workmen in his seven-forge workshop. In addition to his blacksmith business, he served as armorer to the colony and later to the state of Virginia during the Revolutionary War, maintaining weapons for patriot forces. Today, skilled blacksmiths in the shop produce iron and steel tools, hardware, household furnishings, and agricultural implements for the Historic Area, employing the same methods as their eighteenth-century counterparts.

■**King's Arms Barber Shop** (Wigmaker). The wigmaker invites you to his place of business: "To all ladies and gentlemen, we offer all three branches of the trade: wigmaking, barbering, and hairdressing. Using horse, goat, and human hair, our wigmakers craft the finest wigs, curls, and queues for people of fashion. Those so inclined may be pleased that we offer all manner of washing and bathing, along with the finest soaps, perfumes, and powders prepared by the best hands. Counted among our customers are such notables as Thomas Jefferson, Patrick Henry, Peyton Randolph, Thomas Everard, and Peter Pelham."

■**Margaret Hunter Shop** (Milliner). From this shop, between 1771 and 1787, Margaret Hunter, a milliner, both imported and made fashionable accessories. Today, the three clothing trades of milliner, mantua-maker (gown maker), and tailor are demonstrated and inter-

preted here. Learn how these tradesmen and women adapted their businesses, work, and lives to the Revolution.

■**Mary Stith House.** Enjoy special interpretive programs and encounters with "People of the Past" who portray eighteenth-century citizens.

■**Pasteur & Galt Apothecary Shop.** Do you have a fever, toothache, or broken bone? Learn more about eighteenth-century medical theory and treatment and the preparation of medications at the shop of apothecary-surgeons Drs. Pasteur and Galt.

■**Printing Office** and **Bookbindery.** Watch as tradesmen use reproduction printing presses to print copies of colonial newspapers, political notices, and manuals. Printed items such as these played a key role in spreading news and information that influenced the choices Virginians made in the years before and during the Revolution.

■**Raleigh Tavern.** Burgesses and other Virginians gathered at the Raleigh Tavern to discuss the political events that led to revolution. James Southall's tavern also served as a center for social and commercial gatherings—charter members of the Phi Beta Kappa Society met in the Apollo Room—private and public dinners, lectures and exhibitions, and auctions of merchandise, property, and the enslaved. Today at the Raleigh Tavern, you can meet "People of the Past" who portray colonial citizens.

■**Wetherburn's Tavern.** An exhibition in this original building focuses on Henry Wetherburn, his family, and his slaves, who made Wetherburn's Tavern one of the most successful of the 1750s. The outbuildings behind Wetherburn's form a domestic production area essential to the operation of a busy colonial tavern.

SECTION 3
THE CAPITOL AND ITS SURROUNDINGS

■**Ayscough House** (Gunsmith). See gunsmiths fashioning iron, steel, brass, and wood into firearms that are both functional and pleasing to the eye. Discover the importance of rifles, fowling pieces, and muskets to this eighteenth-century community. Learn how

A WORLD TURNED UPSIDE DOWN

There was a rhythm to life in the late colonial period of Williamsburg's history. Nature governed the flow of the day, and established institutions offered a comfortable order that had served the colony well for generations.

By the third quarter of the eighteenth century, all that is changing.

Williamsburg was in the midst of not only a political revolution but also social, religious, consumer, and technological revolutions. The citizens of Williamsburg and the rest of British America were undergoing fundamental changes in the way they lived their lives. Some of the changes they could control. Others were out of their control. They were living in an era where comfortable traditions were being replaced by new ways.

Today, a journey to Colonial Williamsburg's Historic Area is an opportunity to see how a community dealt with these changes. Tour the home of Peyton Randolph and glimpse what Virginians considered fashionable and what it took to run a household. Sit in the House of Burgesses and wrestle with the same issues that led Virginians to rebel against the most powerful nation in the world. Visit a trade shop and marvel at the technical sophistication craftsmen brought to creating objects. Sit face-to-face with one of our character interpreters and learn about a place where, as the title of a popular period tune suggests, "The World Turned Upside Down."

Programs change from season to season and year to year, so call 1-800-HISTORY (447-8679) before you visit to request a calendar of events. If you have access to the Internet, you can learn about daily and special programming at our Web site www.colonialwilliamsburg.org/visit. Once you are in Williamsburg, check your weekly program guide for information on events being offered during your visit.

gunsmiths such as the Geddys and John Brush provided items from gunlocks to tomahawks in a wide range of materials.

■**Capitol.** Stand in the House of Burgesses and imagine Patrick Henry thundering against British taxation. Decide whether you would have voted for—or against—independence.

■**Public Gaol.** Pirates, murderers, thieves, runaway slaves, suspected loyalists, and debtors inhabited the cells at the Public Gaol (pronounced "jail") at one time or another. Imagine living in this "strong sweet Prison," either as a prisoner or as a member of the family of gaolkeeper Peter Pelham.

Tickets, Treasures, and Books. This store offers many historical and nonhistorical publications, games, and guest service items such as cameras and film, as well as admission tickets to all the buildings, carriage rides, and evening programs. The staff of the shop is pleased to direct guests and answer questions regarding their visit to the historic sites and availability of tickets for special programs and to make dining reservations.

SECTION 4
AROUND PALACE GREEN

■**George Wythe House.** Visit the home of Thomas Jefferson's teacher and friend. George Wythe was a prominent attorney, burgess, clerk of the House of Burgesses, signer of the Declaration of Independence, framer of the U.S. Constitution, professor of law, and judge.

■**Weaver.** It was difficult for Virginia weavers to compete with imported goods, but some managed. Explore the technology of weaving and other aspects of textile production, including spinning and dyeing, on the George Wythe House property.

■**Basketmaker.** During much of the year, basketmakers work behind the George Wythe House.

■**Thomas Everard House.** An exhibition features the lives of widower Thomas Everard, his two daughters, and nineteen slaves. Everard arrived in Virginia as an orphan apprentice in the 1730s and rose to the positions of clerk of the York County Court, mayor of Williamsburg, member of the Bruton Parish Church vestry, and deputy clerk of the General Court.

■**Play Booth Theater** (open seasonally). Enjoy scenes from plays performed in Williamsburg in the years immediately before the American Revolution.

SECTION 5
THE GOVERNOR'S PALACE

■**Governor's Palace.** Tour the elegant and imposing residence of seven royal governors.

From the weaponry display in the entrance hall to the royal portraits in the ballroom, the Governor's Palace was meant to impress visitors with the prestige and power of the king's representative in Virginia. During the Revolution, the first two governors of the Commonwealth of Virginia, Patrick Henry and Thomas Jefferson, also lived here.

Explore the beautiful gardens, then visit the kitchen to see demonstrations of eighteenth-century cooking techniques and to learn about dining customs and kitchen duties.

■**Wheelwright.** In the eighteenth century, there was a demand for wheeled vehicles of every kind—wheelbarrows, riding chairs, carriages, and carts. Today, the wheelwrights construct and repair the vehicles used throughout the Historic Area, from riding chairs to cannon carriages.

SECTION 6
FROM PALACE GREEN TO THE COLLEGE OF WILLIAM AND MARY

Bruton Parish Church. There was no separtion of church and state in colonial Virginia. The Church of England was the official religion for the colony, and, as the Anglican church in the capital, Bruton Parish Church was probably the most important church in Virginia. This Episcopal church has been in use since 1715 and serves an active congregation today.

Colonial Garden and Nursery (open seasonally). Learn about eighteenth-century horticultural practices from garden historians, then purchase plants and supplies to create your own colonial-style garden.

James Geddy House and **Foundry.** This house served as the residence, workshop, and shop for silversmith James Geddy Jr. Learn about the domestic and business life of the Geddy family.

In the foundry behind the house, watch skilled craftsmen cast objects in bronze, brass, pewter, and silver.

Shoemaker's Shop. The shoemaker made plain and fancy shoes and boots for gentlemen. Watch as tradesmen hand-sew shoes with "good thread well twisted" and stitches that are "hard drawn with handleathers," as one colonial Virginia statute prescribed.

Taliaferro-Cole Shop (Harnessmaker-Saddler). Leather was one of the most useful raw materials in the eighteenth century. Today, tradesmen make harnesses, saddles, leather water buckets, and other useful goods.

Wren Building. The Wren Building is the oldest academic building still in use in America. Learn about the important role the

College of William and Mary played in the intellectual life of the Virginia colony and the extraordinary number of distinguished alumni, including Thomas Jefferson, John Marshall, and James Monroe, it nurtured.

SECTION 7
NORTH ENGLAND AND NICHOLSON BACK STREETS

Brickyard (open seasonally). Watch and perhaps help as brickmakers tread clay and mold bricks to be fired in a kiln. Although brickyards like this one would have been familiar to eighteenth-century residents, bricks were often made at or near building sites.

Hay's Cabinetmaking Shop. Visit the wareroom—a combination showroom and warehouse—where the cabinetmaker met his customers and conducted the majority of his business. Then go to the workroom and watch the master, journeymen, and apprentices use the hand tools and technology of the colonial era to produce furniture, harpsichords, and spinets.

Peyton Randolph House. What did "revolution" mean to the residents of this stately home? To Speaker of the House of Burgesses Peyton Randolph, it meant leading the patriot movement in Virginia and eventually in Philadelphia, where he served as president of the first and second Continental Congresses. To Peyton's wife, Betty, it meant coping with the British occupation of Williamsburg in 1781, followed by the allied French and American forces before the siege of Yorktown. To several of the Randolph slaves, it meant a chance for freedom by running away to the British.

Robertson's Windmill. Colonial Virginians depended on local mills to grind the grain from which they made their bread, a staple of their diet that appeared at nearly every meal.

■**Great Hopes Plantation.** This site presents life on a middle-class farm. See agricultural, domestic, and carpentry activities of both enslaved and free people.

■**Carpenter.** Eighteenth-century Williamsburg was crowded with carpenters who raised and finished houses, outbuildings, stores, and shops and who oversaw the construction of the numerous impressive public buildings. Today, skilled carpenters prepare building materials at Great Hopes Plantation and construct buildings there and at other sites around the Historic Area.

■**Cooper.** In the Ludwell-Paradise Stable, watch coopers shape and assemble staves to form casks, piggins, and other wooden containers. In an age without cardboard boxes or plastic buckets, people used products made by the cooper in their homes and businesses—including churns to make butter, buckets to carry water, piggins to scoop things out of larger containers, and casks to store and ship cider, grain, and tobacco. During winter months, coopers can be found at the Palace scullery.

SECTION 8
WALLER AND FRANCIS
BACK STREETS

■**Bassett Hall.** Take a tour of the eighteenth-century house that Mr. and Mrs. John D. Rockefeller Jr. adapted for their Williamsburg home. The house remains much as it was when the Rockefellers restored it and furnished it from the mid-1930s to 1948. You can also tour the gardens, which still bloom in the spring and in the fall, just as they did to mark the Rockefellers' seasonal visits.

■**Benjamin Powell House** (open seasonally). Experience everyday life in a middling colonial household. Your children might help make the bed, prepare dinner,

EVENING PROGRAMS

Colonial Williamsburg offers almost as much to do at night as it does during the day. Experience the life of the common soldier at the Magazine. Engage in festivities at the Raleigh Tavern, or laugh at the antics of a traveling troupe of entertainers at the Courthouse. Attend a candlelit concert at the Governor's Palace. Decide the innocence or guilt of the "Virginia Witch." Hear tales of the unexplained as you walk through the long shadows of Williamsburg after dark.

Call 1-800-HISTORY (447-8679) to purchase your evening program tickets before your visit. You can read about evening programs on our Web site, www.colonialwilliamsburg.org/visit, if you have access to the Internet.

After you arrive, you can buy evening program tickets at the Visitor Center; the Lumber House ticket office; Tickets, Treasures, and Books; and the Merchants Square Ticket Office. Check your weekly program guide for more information about events.

CHECKLIST: DINING AND SHOPPING WITHIN WALKING DISTANCE OF THE HISTORIC AREA

SECTION OF THE HISTORIC AREA	DINING	SHOPPING
8. FRANCIS STREET Near the Magazine	Golden Horseshoe Gold Course Clubhouse Williamsburg Inn Williamsburg Lodge	Golden Horseshoe Golf Club—Gold Course Pro Shop Regency Gift Shop at the Williamsburg Inn Gift Shop at the Williamsburg Lodge
Near the Wren Building	Merchants Square Museum Café	WILLIAMSBURG Craft House Everything WILLIAMSBURG Museum Store WILLIAMSBURG Celebrations WILLIAMSBURG At Home

or weed the garden or learn an eighteenth-century game.

■**Public Hospital.** The Public Hospital was the first public institution in British North America devoted exclusively to the care and treatment of the mentally ill. See how the treatment of mental disorders changed from 1773, when the hospital opened, through 1885, when a fire destroyed the colonial buildings. The Public Hospital serves as the entrance to the DeWitt Wallace Decorative Arts Museum and the Abby Aldrich Rockefeller Folk Art Museum.

■**The DeWitt Wallace Decorative Arts Museum.** A description of the museum begins on page 141.

■**Abby Aldrich Rockefeller Folk Art Museum.** A description of the museum begins on page 144.

FOR FAMILIES

Colonial Williamsburg's Historic Area is a wonderful place for children of all ages. For parents, the Historic Area presents a happy challenge: how to choose, among a myriad of places and programs, those that will most entertain your children. Fortunately, it's generally a kid-friendly place, and there's plenty for all ages to see and do. What follows are just a few of the possibilities.

Be sure to pick up "This Week," available at any ticket sales location, for program information and schedules. Openings and activities change daily. Look for the ☻ symbol for family programs.

TIPS

Restrooms. Restrooms are located in the Visitor Center and throughout the Historic Area. Most provide baby changing stations. Family restrooms are located in the east yard of the Governor's Palace and near the bus stop behind the Magazine.

Food and Drink. Immerse yourselves in an eighteenth-century dining experience at any of the taverns in the Historic Area. Chowning's Tavern has the most casual atmosphere. The family entertainment at Chowning's, which runs from 5:00 to 8:00 p.m., includes balladeers leading period sing-alongs and costumed servers teaching you to play period games. Shields Tavern offers light fare for a quick lunch. For a snack during the day, a favorite stop is the Raleigh Tavern Bakery, where you can take out gingerbread, queen's cake, ham biscuits, cider, and other goodies.

Relax. There's more to see in the Historic Area than you'll be able to cover in any one day, even without children. Sometimes, it pays to slow down for awhile. Let the little ones play, as colonial children did, by a burbling brook in one of the many beautiful gardens. As you tour the town, look up at the tavern and trade signs and guess what you might find at the sign of the ship or at the barber pole. Visit the backyards of the Historic Area buildings. How many gates can you find? How far down Duke of Gloucester Street can you go via backyards and without even touching the street?

A blue box indicates that you need an admission ticket to see an attraction.

ATTRACTIONS AND ACTIVITIES

Time Travel. If you walk from the Visitor Center to the Historic Area, rather than take the bus, you will begin by crossing a five-hundred-foot pedestrian bridge. The plaques in the bridge illustrate how life has changed since colonial times and transition you back to the eighteenth century. Just across the bridge you can begin to explore this new time period at Great Hopes Plantation.

Revolutionary City. Your children can not only watch the Revolution—they can join it. This interactive program, which moves around the east end of Duke of Gloucester Street, follows the collapse of royal government and the impact of war on the citizens of Williamsburg. Let the kids linger and talk to some of the characters after a scene is done.

Fife and Drums. Fifers and drummers, usually boys between ten and eighteen, supported the army in the field. Today, you can enjoy the music of boys and girls in the renowned Fifes and Drums of Colonial Williamsburg as they march through the streets of the Historic Area.

Rare Breeds. Found in pastures, paddocks, chicken coops, and dovecotes, these aren't your ordinary farm animals. Red Devon cattle, Leicester Longwool sheep, American Cream Draft horses, and a variety of feathered friends are among the rare breeds of domestic animals preserved here, all of which bring

another aspect of the past to life. How many animals can you find?

Carriage and Wagon Rides. Tickets are available on the day of the ride at any ticket sales location. Buy your tickets early as these often sell out.

Costume Rentals. Colonial costumes are available for boys and girls at the Visitor Center and at the Market Square stands (open seasonally).

■**Play Booth Theater.** Weather permitting, the Virginia Company of Comedians presents scenes from eighteenth-century theater, musical entre-acts, and theatrical dances once performed during fair days at booths much like this one.

Evening Programs. Would you rather attend a palace ball or the Grand Medley of Entertainments, an eighteenth-century variety show? Among the most popular programs for older kids are "Cry Witch" and ghost tours, though these may be too scary for younger children. Special program tickets are required.

■**Museums of Colonial Williamsburg.** The DeWitt Wallace Decorative Arts Museum and Abby Aldrich Rockefeller Folk Art Museum offer gallery guides, family packs, and family programs. Or you and the kids can explore on your own. With younger children, you can search for certain objects such as animals, favorite colors, or items made from wood. Older kids may want to bring a sketch pad and pencil or buy postcards to send home. The "Down on the Farm" exhibit, which places folk art masterpieces in a farm setting, is especially child friendly. The museum has a café.

VISITING THE HISTORIC SITES

■**Magazine** and **Guardhouse.** For kids who love to play soldier, here's where they can see real guns, muskets, powder, and other military supplies. When British troops snuck into the Magazine and stole the colonists' stockpiles, the incident ignited the Revolution in Virginia.

Courthouse. Older kids will enjoy acting as plaintiffs, defendants, jurors, and the audience for mock trials based on colonial cases. Children can experience firsthand the punishment for stealing a pig by placing necks, hands, and feet in the pillory and stocks just outside the Courthouse. Older kids will also want to see the Public Gaol where Blackbeard's henchmen were imprisoned.

Peyton Randolph House. Witness how the political views of this Revolutionary leader split his family, as well as the families of the slaves who worked here.

Benjamin Powell House. One of the most interactive sites for children, who can join in various eighteenth-century activities. In the dining room, for example, they may learn the proper way to lay a table and serve dinner. In the bedchamber, the horsehair and down mattresses may need airing. In the parlor, they may learn the latest dance steps or make marbles or sweet scent bags. And there are hoops and sticks, tabletop bowls, trapball, lawn bowling, and board and card games to play.

George Wythe House. Your kids would be lucky to have a teacher like George Wythe, whose pupils included Thomas Jefferson and John Marshall. At his house, junior interpreters sometimes demonstrate lawn bowling, hoops and sticks, stilts, and board games like nine man's morris and mancala. Interpreters tell about both gentry children who visited the house and the slave children who lived on the property. The site is also home to several varieties of rare breed chickens, and there are sometimes sheep and horses in the pasture out back.

James Geddy House. Do you have a tough time getting your kids to do chores? Learn how James Geddy Jr.'s children were a part of his business as well as his household, and discover how this tradesman's family was affected by the Revolution. Children can play with wooden hoops, tops, clay marbles, and other colonial toys.

Great Hopes Plantation. Williamsburg was the capital city, but the majority of Virginians lived on small farms, or "plantations," to use the eighteenth-century word. A visit to Great Hopes gives you a glimpse into the lives and livelihoods of a rural family and its enslaved workers. You may be able to watch carpenters constructing an outbuilding or farmers plow-

ing the fields with oxen. Children can sometimes work in the garden, visit the kitchen, and split wood as they learn about daily life and work on a rural plantation.

Governor's Palace. A tour of the Palace may seem a bit daunting for very young children, but there are things that can catch their interest. Visit the kitchen to find out what the governor, such as Lord Dunmore or Patrick Henry, and his family might be having for dinner. Explore the maze, but don't get lost in it!

VISITING THE TRADES

Blacksmith. The blacksmiths are going at it hammer and tongs, to say nothing of files and rasps. Fire, smoke, hot irons—everything you've warned your children to stay away from, so how could they resist?

Brickyard. The brickyard may be the

most kid-friendly site in Colonial Williamsburg's Historic Area. Kids love the huge mud hole, the treading pit. There they can take off their shoes, step into the slippery mire, and mix clay and water with their feet to prepare the raw material of bricks.

Millliner. Visit the Margaret Hunter Shop and plan your wardrobe for the year. The milliner has filled her shelves with the finest of imported fashions and household items.

Wigmaker. First, shave your head. Then, let us know whether you'd prefer human, horse, goat, or yak hair.

James Geddy Foundry. Watch the founders turn molten metal into spoons, candlesticks, and sword handles. Help pump the bellows.

ON THE WEB

All sorts of children's activities and games can be found online at www.colonialwilliams burg.org/kids.

WASHINGTON, HENRY, AND
JEFFERSON IN WILLIAMSBURG

Williamsburg was a training ground for George Washington, Patrick Henry, and Thomas Jefferson. Each came here as a young man, and each matured here as a statesman.

George Washington's first known trip to Williamsburg was in 1752. Late that year, Governor Dinwiddie commissioned the young man adjutant of the Southern District of Virginia. Washington attracted further public notice in 1754, when he returned to Williamsburg after completing a dangerous mission to the Ohio country. This feat launched the twenty-one-year-old Washington's military career, which he later parlayed into a seat in the House of Burgesses. In 1759, he married Martha Dandridge Custis, a wealthy widow with many relatives in and around Williamsburg. His experiences during his sixteen years as a burgess—negotiating legislation in committee rooms, engaging in political discussions in Williamsburg's homes and taverns, forging social and political relationships—helped mold him into a political leader.

Patrick Henry first traveled to Williamsburg in 1760 to obtain a law license. Henry began making a name for himself as an attorney and gained even greater fame when, as a first-time burgess, he led Virginia's opposition to the Stamp Act in 1765. His impassioned "Caesar had . . . his Brutus" speech provoked cries of treason from the other legislators, but the House adopted most of Henry's resolutions against the Stamp Act. For the next eleven years, Henry's ringing oratory—including his immortal cry, "Give me liberty or give me death!"—rallied Virginians to the patriot cause. Henry himself took up arms in the summer of 1775 when the Virginia Convention elected him colonel of the first regiment.

Thomas Jefferson arrived in Williamsburg in 1760 at the age of seventeen to attend the College of William and Mary. After two years at the college, Jefferson began reading law under George Wythe. He also attended the courts and legislative sessions at the Capitol and was standing near the door of the House of Burgesses when Henry delivered his Caesar-Brutus speech.

Jefferson was elected to the House of Burgesses in 1769. His first session was as eventful as Henry's had been four years earlier. After Lord Botetourt, Virginia's royal governor, dissolved the legislature for protesting the Townshend Acts, the burgesses met at the Raleigh Tavern and drew up a nonimportation agreement. Jefferson signed the agreement, as did Washington and Henry.

In the years that followed, all three men supported the patriot cause and the nation that grew out of it. Each represented Virginia at the Continental Congress in Philadelphia, although not at the same time. Washington led the American forces to victory over the British and guided the country as our first president. Henry served as the first governor of the state of Virginia, eventually holding that office five times. Jefferson wrote the Declaration of Independence, succeeded Henry as governor, and ultimately served as president of the United States.

THE HISTORIC AREA
STREET BY STREET

The following pages discuss the history of the buildings and sites in the Historic Area as well as "Becoming Americans," the interpretative basis for the story we tell. The section numbers correspond to those on the map on pages 26–27. Each section contains one or more detailed maps, drawings of the buildings, and character sketches that are based on real people and combine fact and conjecture. Please note, an asterisk indicates that a building is an original eighteenth- or nineteenth-century structure, and a blue box indicates that you need an admission ticket to see an attraction.

You can tour each section of the Historic Area independently and in any order. Each area map's symbols will enable you to identify and locate the following:

- exhibitions requiring a ticket.
- original buildings.
- places to shop.
- places to dine.
- exhibition gardens.
- information and ticket sales sites.
- restrooms.
- cold drinks.
- water fountains.
- public telephones.
- other services and places to visit.
- facilities accessible to those with disabilities.

LOOKING NORTH

PALACE STREET

N. ENGLAND STREET

*St. George Tucker House

*Grissell Hay Lodging House

*Peyton Randolph House

NICHOLSON STREET

MARKET SQUARE

STREET

D *Roscow Cole House

*Courthouse

Chowning's Tavern

DUKE OF GLOUCESTER STREET

*Market Square Tavern

*Greenhow Brick Office

Market Square stands

*Magazine

Guardhouse

QUEEN

C R D

FRANCIS STREET

S. ENGLAND STREET

SECTION

1

Market Square

Section 1	R Restrooms
Admission Ticket Required	C Public Telephones
Places to Shop	D Cold Drinks
Other Places to Visit	▲ Water Fountains
Exhibition Gardens	X Buy Tickets Here
Places to Dine	* Original Building
Lodging	♿ Accessible to Those with Disabilities
Services or Privately Occupied	

0   100   200   300   400   500 FEET

MARKET SQUARE

An asterisk indicates that a building is an original eighteenth- or nineteenth-century structure. A blue box indicates that you need an admission ticket to see an attraction.

Market Square, a green open space about halfway between the College of William and Mary and the Capitol, was set aside as a permanent area for markets and fairs by an act of the General Assembly early in the eighteenth century.

There, before dawn on each market day—as often as six times a week later in the century—the town slowly came alive. People from nearby farms brought produce in creaking wagons or carts. Sometimes cattle and sheep competed for road space leading to the square, driven on by shouting children and yelping dogs. In the predawn light, vendors unloaded meat, eggs, milk, butter, fish, crabs, oysters, fruit, and vegetables, displaying their wares on makeshift counters of pine boards.

Armed with lists of the provisions needed for the day, housewives, cooks, and kitchen slaves selected the freshest eggs, the ripest peaches, and the choicest cuts of meat. Shopping was an everyday chore in an age without refrigeration.

By midmorning, most of the produce had been sold or looked shopworn. The crowds began to melt away. Some of the farmers repaired to one of the taverns conveniently located next to the square to relax, listen to the local gossip, and quench their thirst.

The Williamsburg charter of 1722 established two fairs each year, one on April 23, the feast of St. George, the patron saint of England, and the other on December 12. A variety of merchandise, including livestock,

was sold on the square. People enjoyed games, puppet shows, horse races, cockfights, dancing and fiddling for prizes, and a chase for a "Pig, with the Tail soap'd."

Auctions of the enslaved, goods, and land occurred on Market Square. After Josiah Chowning's death in 1772, for example, some property that he owned and one of his slaves were auctioned off in front of the Courthouse—within sight of the tavern that bears his name.

Market Square was also important as a seat of local government. In 1715, the courthouse for James City County was built there. The present structure, built at the center of the square in 1770, housed both the municipal and the county courts until 1932. In all, a local government building stood on or adjacent to the square for more than two hundred years.

Near the Courthouse was the training field for the Williamsburg Militia Company, which mustered there several times a year. With a few exceptions, the colonial militia consisted of every free, white, able-bodied man age sixteen to sixty. A militia muster brought together members of different social classes without leveling social distinctions. Musters formalized and validated the authority figures in colonial society, the large landowners who were appointed to command the militia and who served without pay. Those officers deemed military service both an honor and an obligation, and they could be fined as much as twenty pounds for failure to perform. By contrast, three shillings was the typical fine for an absent militiaman.

Much of the rest of the local population turned out to watch the training and drills in quick loading and shooting. All was not marching and manual-of-arms practice, however. Militiamen participated in foot races, wrestling matches, and cudgeling standoffs, with prizes being awarded to the victors.

Afterward, officers customarily treated the entire company to a hogshead of rum punch.

Market Square's central location made it a favorite place for public notices, official announcements, communal celebrations, and elections. In July 1746, a large bonfire was lit and the public consumed three barrels of punch in honor of the Duke of Cumberland's victory over Bonnie Prince Charlie at the Battle of Culloden in Scotland. On July 25,

MEET . . . JANE MOODY

Early mornings found Jane Moody and other middling housewives shopping for their households in Market Square. They purchased milk, butter, vegetables, fruits, fresh meats, and other foodstuffs. Because Jane and her husband, Matthew, kept a tavern at their house, she had to buy supplies for both her family and their customers.

Running a tavern was much like managing a home, only on a larger scale. The Moodys' house on Capitol Landing Road was nearly always crowded with tavern customers, usually travelers waiting for or just arrived on the ferry from Gloucester County that Matthew Moody operated. Four slaves did the heaviest work. The two women, Thomasin and Rachel, saw to most of the cooking and cleaning. Cutty and London took care of customers' horses and helped with the ferry service. Sometimes Matthew hired ferrymen to assist him. Occasionally his grown-up sons pitched in to keep the family business going.

Responsibilities for operating the tavern fell mostly to Jane these days. No longer the lively sixty-year-old widower she had married, Matthew was getting on in years now. Jane found it both convenient and reassuring that her stepsons Philip, Ishmael, William, and Matthew Jr. lived nearby. Her stepsons were kind to her and solicitous of their aging father, and Jane felt no resentment toward them. She wished her own children could help, but they lived too far away.

Jane enjoyed living in Williamsburg. In addition to the convenience of the twice-weekly market, town life offered other advantages. Once in a while, Jane drank tea with her women friends in her neighborhood. She visited Mr. Greenhow's store to purchase necessities for the house and tavern as well as the occasional luxury for herself—a skein of silk or a handkerchief. When Matthew was not feeling well, he could consult one of several local doctors. Jane looked forward to worshipping at Bruton Parish Church, her major consolation. Before and after Sunday services, she enjoyed chatting with acquaintances.

Although Jane occasionally longed for a quiet moment to call her own, she knew how lucky she was to have an honest husband, helpful relatives close at hand, a profitable business, and a good roof over her head.

■ *Courthouse

1776, attorney Benjamin Waller proclaimed the Declaration of Independence from the Courthouse steps to a huge throng after the news arrived from Philadelphia.

Elections were public affairs in colonial Virginia. Voters gathered at the Courthouse to choose by voice vote the men who would serve as their representatives in the House of Burgesses.

Market Square's convenient location must have been paramount in the decision to keep there the town's fire engine, which was in use by 1756. Fire was a constant hazard in the eighteenth century. An efficient response to the threat of fire required organization and cooperation.

Market Square is dominated by the ■ Courthouse. Built in 1770–1771, the Courthouse was the meeting place for the James City County Court, the Hustings Court (the municipal court for the city of Williamsburg), and the mayor and aldermen of the City Council for more than 150 years. Like many other Virginia courthouses, it is T-shaped. Its formal design elements—round-headed windows, a cantilevered pediment, and an octagonal cupola with the original weather vane—add to and reinforce the building's official appearance.

In colonial Virginia, the county court was the principal agent of local government and had broad executive and judicial authority. Its jurisdiction included crimes ranging from petty theft to absence from church. Free subjects of the king accused of felonies were sent on to the General Court, which met in the Capitol; slaves were tried in county courts for the same crimes. If convicted, both were publicly hanged as punishment and as a warning to others. The municipal court, known as the Hustings Court, possessed the civil jurisdiction within the city of

Roscow Cole House

Williamsburg that the James City County Court exercised in the adjacent county.

The Hustings Court met on the first Monday of each month, and the James City County Court convened on the second Monday. Sessions lasted several days until the backlog of cases was cleared.

The onlookers who often filled the Courthouse to overflowing on court days got their fill of debtor and creditor tales, card cheaters, pig stealers, and more. The theatricality of the proceedings was heightened because minor offenders were usually punished immediately after the verdict. Often their sentences included public flogging at the whipping post conveniently located just outside the Courthouse. Petty offenders were locked in the stocks or pillories where they were exposed to public ridicule and abuse.

The ■**Magazine** was erected in 1715 after Lieutenant Governor Alexander Spotswood urgently requested a "good substantial house of brick" in which to store the arms and ammunition dispatched from London for the defense of the colony. Governor Spotswood himself is credited with the Magazine's unusual octagonal design.

The Magazine assumed added importance during the French and Indian War, 1754–1763, when for the first time the colony supported large-scale military operations in the Ohio Valley, territory that the Crown claimed under the Virginia charter of 1609. Because the amount of gunpowder in storage exceeded sixty thousand pounds, the residents of Williamsburg felt that the Magazine needed further protection. A high wall was therefore built around the Magazine and a ■**Guardhouse** was constructed nearby.

At its busiest, the Magazine probably contained two to three thousand Brown Bess muskets and enough shot, powder, and flints to equip a formidable army. Other military equipment—tents, tools, swords, pikes, canteens, and cooking utensils—was also stored in the Magazine.

During the night of April 20–21, 1775, British sailors acting on royal governor Lord Dunmore's orders removed gunpowder from the Magazine. Although violence was averted, the Gunpowder Incident helped move Virginians toward revolution.

Greenhow Brick Office

After the Revolution, an arsenal at Williamsburg was no longer needed, although Confederate forces did store powder in the Magazine during the Civil War. At various times, the building was used as a market, a Baptist meetinghouse, a dancing school, and finally a livery stable.

The Association for the Preservation of Virginia Antiquities (APVA) made the safeguarding of the Magazine its first project. In 1986, Colonial Williamsburg obtained the Magazine from the APVA.

Directly west of the Magazine is the **Greenhow Brick Office.** Although Williamsburg was the port of entry for the upper James River, there was no customhouse in town, a situation much belabored by the inspector general of customs when he visited in 1760. Accounts indicate that a public building, "located in the square" on municipal property, existed by 1764. It is likely that this modest brick structure was used as the Williamsburg customhouse.

The brick portion of the **Roscow Cole House** was erected in 1812 to face Market Square by Roscow Cole, a local merchant. The westerly wooden frame section is a reconstruction of an eighteenth-century building. An 1830 insurance policy called this structure a dry goods store.

The **St. George Tucker House** belonged to noted jurist St. George Tucker, who attended the College of William and Mary and later became professor of law there. Tucker bought the property in 1788. He moved an older

building, which had faced Palace Green, to this site, enlarged the house, and reoriented it toward Market Square.

Today the St. George Tucker House is Colonial Williamsburg's donor reception center. Through the generosity of Mr. and Mrs. James W. Gorman, Ms. Marilyn Brown and Mr. Douglas N. Morton, and an anonymous donor, the house has been restored to its eighteenth-century appearance and redecorated

■ *Guardhouse*

■ **Magazine*

St. George Tucker House

with period reproductions. At the St. George Tucker House, conveniently located in the Historic Area, donors to the Foundation can rest and enjoy light refreshments. The staff assists with reservations and information. Guests also enjoy visiting with other friends of the Foundation.

The **Grissell Hay Lodging House** to the east may be one of the first houses on Market Square. The core of the house may date from around 1720, when it belonged to Dr. Archibald Blair, a Scottish physician and a partner in Williamsburg's leading mercantile business, the Prentis Store. The present exterior probably dates from the second half of the eighteenth century. Apothecary Peter Hay, whose shop on Duke of Gloucester Street burned in 1756, lived here in the 1760s. After Hay's death, his widow, Grissell, operated the dwelling as a lodging house. Widows who needed to support themselves and their children often kept lodging houses (the equivalents of today's bed-and-breakfasts).

■**Peyton Randolph House.** A description of the house begins on page 111.

Chowning's Tavern stands east of the Courthouse. In 1766, Josiah Chowning advertised the opening of his tavern "where all who please to favour me with their custom may depend on the best of entertainment for themselves, servants, and horses, and good pasturage." Chowning's Tavern serves hearty fare similar to the dishes enjoyed by its patrons in the eighteenth century.

Across the street, **Market Square Tavern** has been a hostelry for more than two hundred years. Its most celebrated lodger was Thomas Jefferson, who rented rooms there from Thomas Craig, tailor, while he studied law under George Wythe. Neither Chowning's nor Market Square Tavern, however, could compete with the more profitable establishments farther east down Duke of Gloucester Street toward the Capitol. Today, Market Square Tavern and the Market Square Tavern Kitchen are two of several of Colonial Williamsburg's hotel facilities located in the Historic Area.

Chowning's Tavern

Grissell Hay Lodging House

Becoming Americans
Our Struggle to Be Both Free and Equal

FAMILY LIFE

In the 1700s, changes in traditional family structures affected the way family members defined themselves in relation to one another and to society. Ultimately, these changes created the pattern for the "modern American" family.

Adverse conditions in seventeenth-century Virginia made it difficult for European and African immigrants to form stable family structures but began to ease by the late 1600s. Native American families, however, continued to be undermined by disease, displacement, and warfare.

The European family was modeled after a patriarchal ideal that placed the father in a position of supreme authority over an extended family. Reality often differed from the ideal. Enslaved Africans, torn from their homelands and denied the stability of legal marriage, created distinctively African-Virginian family structures that relied on African concepts of extended kinships. European observers misunderstood the traditional patterns of Native American work and family relationships. Interaction with Europeans further altered the family structure of Native American families and ultimately threatened their very survival.

A more openly affectionate, child-centered family that reflected egalitarian republican sentiment and changing roles for men and women began to emerge in gentry and middling white families in the late 1700s. This redefined structure became part of the ideal for the new American nation, yet lack of opportunity continued for many white and most Native American and black families.

Market Square Tavern

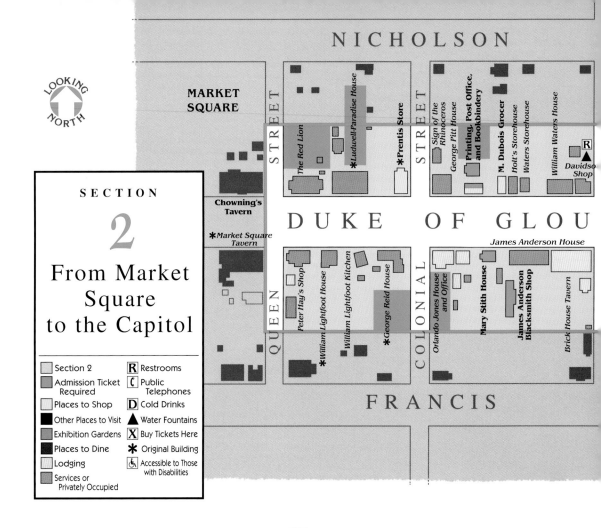

NICHOLSON STREET

MARKET SQUARE

Ludwell-Paradise House

The Red Lion

Prentis Store

Sign of the Rhinoceros

George Pitt House

Printing, Post Office, and Bookbindery

M. Dubois Grocer

Holt's Storehouse

Waters Storehouse

William Waters House

R Davidso Shop

Chowning's Tavern

Market Square Tavern

DUKE OF GLOU

James Anderson House

Peter Hay's Shop

William Lightfoot House

William Lightfoot Kitchen

George Reid House

Orlando Jones House and Office

Mary Stith House

James Anderson Blacksmith Shop

Brick House Tavern

QUEEN STREET

COLONIAL

FRANCIS

SECTION

2

From Market Square to the Capitol

▢ Section 2	**R**	Restrooms
▢ Admission Ticket Required	**C**	Public Telephones
▢ Places to Shop	**D**	Cold Drinks
■ Other Places to Visit	▲	Water Fountains
▢ Exhibition Gardens	**X**	Buy Tickets Here
■ Places to Dine	✱	Original Building
▢ Lodging	♿	Accessible to Those with Disabilities
▢ Services or Privately Occupied		

FROM MARKET SQUARE TO THE CAPITOL

An asterisk indicates that a building is an original eighteenth- or nineteenth-century structure. A blue box indicates that you need an admission ticket to see an attraction.

Attracted by the numerous opportunities to eat, drink, or socialize, or perhaps to purchase the latest goods from London or a newspaper or book, most eighteenth-century townsfolk and visitors to the colonial capital found their way "downtown" on Duke of Gloucester Street.

The three blocks of Duke of Gloucester Street from Market Square eastward to the Capitol were the busiest in eighteenth-century Williamsburg. General stores and specialty shops offered a wide range of goods at prices that ordinary consumers could afford. A number of taverns provided food, drink, and accommodations to an increasingly mobile and widely traveled public. In 1765, one visitor described the scene: "In the Day time people hurrying back and forwards from the Capitol

STREET

STREET

D C

Prentis House

Russell House

★Margaret Hunter Shop (Milliner)

The Golden Ball (Silversmith)

Unicorn's Horn and John Carter's Store

Raleigh Tavern Kitchen and Bakery

★Alexander Craig House

Scrivener Store

Pasteur & Galt Apothecary Shop

★Nicolson Store

John Crump House

Edinburgh Castle Tavern

See Section 3
page 66

★Secretary's Office
Tickets, Treasures, and Books   X

Capitol

Raleigh Tavern

C E S T E R   S T R E E T

★Wetherburn's Tavern   King's Arms Tavern

BOTETOURT STREET

Tarpley's Store

★Charlton House

King's Arms Barber Shop (Wigmaker)

Alexander Purdie House

John Coke Office

Shields Tavern

★Palmer House

BLAIR STREET

C
D

STREET

0   100   200   300   400   500 FEET

to the taverns, and at night, Carousing and Drinking in one Chamber and box and Dice in another, which Continues till morning."

Today, these blocks of Duke of Gloucester Street appear more neatly residential than they would have some two hundred years ago when many of the houses served interchangeably as shops, stores, taverns, and residences and the street bustled with mercantile activity. Lots at the end of the street nearest the Capitol had the most commercial character. They increased in value and often were subdivided as retailers and tavern keepers jostled for a location in this popular area.

William Parks, the first public printer in the colony of Virginia, began the weekly *Virginia Gazette* in 1736. Williamsburg thus became a communications center as news of the world, of the colonies, and of the city provided essential information to those whose affairs depended more and more on the "freshest advices" from far and near.

The Revolutionary War spurred industrial development behind the James Anderson House, where blacksmith and armorer James Anderson oversaw the public armory. The armorer's shop repaired weapons and provided military hardware for patriot forces from 1775 to 1780, when the capital, and James Anderson, relocated to Richmond.

The Red Lion

*Ludwell-Paradise House

FROM MARKET SQUARE TO COLONIAL STREET

This part of Duke of Gloucester Street was less commercially attractive than the east end because it was farther from the Capitol. As a result, the block's half-acre lots were never subdivided. **The Red Lion** on the left suffered many failures and a rapid turnover of its tavern keepers, including Josiah Chowning at one time.

The haystack sign announces **Peter Hay's Shop.** Apothecary Hay fared somewhat better as a businessman than did his neighbors across the street until April 1756 when, the *Maryland Gazette* reported, a fire broke out in his shop "and in less than Half an Hour entirely consumed the same, together with all Medicines, Utensils, & c." Fortunately, "the Assistance of a Fire Engine" prevented damage to nearby buildings. The kitchen behind the shop is now a hotel accommodation.

The **Ludwell-Paradise House** is an example of the mixed use of buildings over time.

Although an earlier structure existed on this site, the present dwelling was built by Philip Ludwell III about 1755. In Williamsburg, space meant money, so even this elegant town house was rented for many years. William Rind—and later his widow, Clementina—operated a press on the premises. Ludwell's eccentric daughter, Lucy Ludwell Paradise, lived here in the 1800s. The Ludwell-Paradise House was the first property purchased by John D. Rockefeller Jr.

The **William Lightfoot House** and **Kitchen** on the south side of the street belonged to a Yorktown merchant whose business apparently brought him to Williamsburg so often that he felt the need for a local dwelling.

The **George Reid House** may have been built as late as 1790 by a merchant who operated a store near the Capitol. Archaeological excavations revealed that a path near the house was paved with fragments of clay pipes that might have been broken in shipment to Williamsburg. Matching pieces have also been found at the Prentis Store across the street.

The **Prentis Store** is Williamsburg's best

*George Reid House

William Lightfoot Kitchen

*William Lightfoot House

Prentis Store

surviving example of a colonial store. The firm of Prentis and Company operated a highly successful general store in this handsome original building from 1740 until the Revolution.

A classic example of store architecture, its gable end faces the street. Through the door above, merchandise could easily be lifted into the loft. Windows along the sides were located toward the rear of the building to light the counting room and to leave long, blank walls for ample shelving in the sales area.

The Prentis Store dates from 1739 to 1740. It survived well into the twentieth century as an automobile service station, which partially explains why so few changes were made to the building: it was likely considered "beneath" modernization or conversion. Prentis himself lived a block away in a substantial house at the corner of Botetourt and Duke of Gloucester Streets, where he spent his leisure hours planning and planting a fine garden. Today's Prentis Store offers handcrafted items made by the Historic Trades shops using authentic eighteenth-century tools and methods.

Peter Hay's Shop

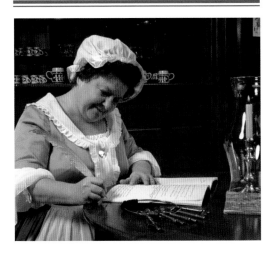

MEET . . . JANE VOBE

For more than thirty years, until about 1785, Jane Vobe operated the King's Arms Tavern in Williamsburg. Vobe was one of several female tavern keepers in town. Hers was a place, according to a French traveler, "where all the best people resorted," a communications hub and the site of many important dinners and political meetings.

In May 1757, George Washington recorded that he paid "Expenses at Mrs. Vobes," and he continued to patronize her place regularly through 1774. Burgesses, councillors, the governor, and locals alike frequented the tavern. While going about her business, Vobe observed (and undoubtedly overheard) the conversations of such Revolutionary figures as Peyton Randolph and Baron von Steuben.

Among Vobe's enslaved workers was Gowan Pamphlet, who later became a Baptist preacher and a leader of his people. He was manumitted after Vobe's death.

Vobe's tavern was originally on Waller Street east of the Capitol. By February 1772, she had opened the King's Arms Tavern opposite the Raleigh Tavern. At some point during the Revolution, her tavern was renamed "The Eagle."

Sign of the
Rhinoceros

George Pitt House

■ *Printing Office, Post Office,*
and ■*Bookbindery*

*M. Dubois
Grocer*

FROM COLONIAL STREET TO BOTETOURT STREET

Although the **George Pitt House** was built as a residence, it sometimes served as a combination shop and dwelling in the eighteenth century. Sarah Packe, a young widow, had her millinery business here and also took in lodgers. Later, Dr. George Pitt purchased the property and opened an apothecary shop, the **Sign of the Rhinoceros**. Dr. Pitt sold the property to printer John Dixon in 1774.

Next door, the ■**Printing Office, Post Office,** and ■**Bookbindery** were the town's communications hub. The boxlike protruding windows decorated with the most recent prints from England not only proclaimed the latest fashions but also helped to create a demand for them. Reading was recognized as an important element in commerce. The newspapers, prints, magazines, Bibles, and inexpensive books on every conceivable

subject available here fueled the great information explosion of the eighteenth century.

William Parks published the *Virginia Gazette,* the first newspaper printed in the colony, from 1736 to 1750. He also became "public printer" to the General Assembly and the colony's first postmaster. Parks established a paper mill just outside Williamsburg—"the first Mill of the Kind, that ever was erected in this Colony." In that venture, he had the advice and backing of fellow printer Benjamin Franklin, who later purchased paper from Parks's mill. Succeeding printers used the site until 1780, when the government moved to Richmond.

Several hundred pieces of type, probably Dutch, were unearthed at this site during archaeological excavations that also uncovered bookbinder's ornaments and crucibles in which Parks may have melted lead. Archaeologists also found lead border ornaments used in printing paper money during the French and Indian War.

The next three structures—**M. Dubois Grocer, Holt's Storehouse,** and **Waters Storehouse**—form a fine collection of reconstructed eighteenth-century commercial properties, all of which present their gable ends to the street.

Tenant grocer M. Dubois occupied this store in the late 1770s. Today, M. Dubois Grocer carries food products such as Virginia ham, peanuts, condiments, preserves, and beverages.

The three sugar loaves hanging outside

Holt's Storehouse   *Waters Storehouse*   *William Waters House*   *Davidson Shop*

Holt's Storehouse are the traditional sign of the grocer. In addition to groceries, John Holt sold dry goods and china.

Storekeepers tried to stock a wide range of products, especially yard goods and iron tools. Customers were hard to attract and harder to keep. One local merchant wrote to his Scottish supplier imploring him to send a variety of merchandise, lest the shopkeeper lose the goodwill of his customers: "I find there will be an Absollute Necessity of allways [having] a good assortment in order to keep my Customers entirely to myself without allowing them to go to my neighbours for trifles."

The reconstructed **William Waters House** is named for the wealthy planter from the Eastern Shore who bought the dwelling for his house in town when he moved to Williamsburg about 1750.

The **Davidson Shop** on the corner was once the apothecary shop of Robert Davidson, a "Practitioner in Physick" and mayor of Williamsburg in 1738.

Orlando Jones, born in 1681, owned the original **Orlando Jones House** and **Office** on the south side of the street. His granddaughter Martha Custis married a rising politician, George Washington. The house, office, and kitchen are now hotel guest accommodations.

Mary Stith, daughter of William Stith, president of the College of William and Mary from 1752 to 1755, owned the small structure that is known as the ■**Mary Stith House.** In her will of 1813, she left this lot, its buildings, and much of her estate to her former slaves in gratitude for past services. Today, guests to this reconstructed building enjoy special interpretive programs and encounters with "People of the Past," who portray eighteenth-century citizens.

Next door is the **James Anderson House,** a site that served at various times as a residence and place of business for a tavern keeper, a milliner, a barber and wigmaker, and a chandler and soap boiler before Anderson purchased the property in 1770. Anderson lived at the corner of Francis and Botetourt Streets on the adjoining half lot. He probably purchased this property to accommodate his expanding business.

Behind the house is the ■**James Anderson Blacksmith Shop.** With the exception of the years 1780–1782, when he relocated the business to Richmond following his primary customer, the state government, Anderson operated a blacksmith and armorer's shop here from the 1770s until he died in 1798. During the Revolutionary War, Anderson contracted with the Commonwealth of Virginia to do armorer's work, including cleaning and repairing muskets, swords, and bayonets and manufacturing nails, axes, tomahawks, and vehicle hardware.

This reconstructed shop is one of several buildings associated with the prosperous industrial site. Extensive archaeological excavations revealed the foundations of the forges and workshop, and the building was reconstructed in the mid-1980s using techniques common in the eighteenth century. Construction details were based on thorough field studies of surviving eighteenth-century structures that reflect the style typical of agricultural buildings of the period.

Inside the shop are tools and materials typical of a blacksmith's business in the colonial period. Coal-fired forges and hammers, anvils, files, saws, punches, chisels, and many other tools are used to shape iron and steel into useful articles. The smiths who work here today reproduce iron objects using technology that would have been familiar to James Anderson and his workmen. The shop's segmented appearance and coarse construction reflect the rapid growth of a purely industrial building in response to increased wartime demands for ironwork.

Next door, the **Brick House Tavern** was built as a rental property in the early 1760s. Itinerant tradesmen and others with services or goods to sell would arrange for lodging here, advertise in the *Virginia Gazette,* and show their wares to customers in their rooms. If business seemed promising, they might settle down elsewhere in town; if not, they would move on. Over time, a surgeon, jeweler, watch repairer, milliner, wigmaker, and several tavern keepers, to name a few, called the Brick House Tavern home. Today, it is a hotel facility, as is the Brick House Tavern Shop behind it.

FROM BOTETOURT STREET TO THE CAPITOL

Tarpley's Store, a commercial establishment, is located on the south side of the street.

Brick House Tavern   *James Anderson House*

Merchant James Tarpley erected and operated his store on this lot after it was subdivided in 1759. Newspaper advertisements show that local residents considered this block "the most public part of the city" and "the most convenient spot . . . for trade." Later in the century, Alexander Purdie published a second *Virginia Gazette* here. Purdie's newspaper bore the motto "Always for Liberty, and the Publick Good." He was appointed public printer just before the Revolution. Merchandise typical of that sold in the eighteenth century is available at Tarpley's Store.

Across the street, two residences, the **Prentis House** and the **Russell House,** break up the otherwise commercial character of the block.

The ■**Margaret Hunter Shop,** an original structure, occupies a favorable spot on the busy "downtown" end of the main street.

Typical of commercial buildings, it has a gable-end facade, and its interior is divided between a large unheated storefront and a smaller counting office with a fireplace in the rear. Like many buildings, this one served as both workplace and home for its occupants.

Margaret Hunter first rented and later owned this shop. The eighteenth-century **milliner** made diverse and stylish accessories for men, women, and children and imported and sold fashionable items including the "laces, stockings, jewellery, childbed linens, gentlemen's embroidered wastecoat patterns, and fine hyson tea" that Hunter advertised in 1774.

Today, the **mantua-maker** (gown maker) and **tailor** also practice in this shop. Both these trades profited by cutting and sewing clothing for persons of all rank, from the fine silks of gentlemen and ladies to the rugged linens and woolens of field slaves. The clothing trades together employed the greatest number of artisans in most eighteenth-century cities.

■**The Golden Ball** was the address of James Craig, a jeweler and silversmith from London who established his business at this location in 1765. Craig once made a pair of earrings for Patsy Custis, the stepdaughter of George Washington. In 1772, Craig added a watchmaker to his staff and began advertising his store as "The Golden Ball," a trademark commonly used by jewelers and goldsmiths.

■ *James Anderson Blacksmith Shop*

■ *Mary Stith House*

Orlando Jones Office and *House*

Prentis House

Russell House

■*Margaret Hunter Shop* (Milliner)

Craig lived and worked on these premises with his family of five and one slave until he died in the early 1790s.

The original building on this site was built in 1724 and survived until 1907. A photograph, archaeological excavations of the foundations, and the recollections of former residents guided the reconstruction. Today, skilled **silversmiths** create beautiful objects by hand on the west side of the Golden Ball, and silver hollowware and gold and silver jewelry are sold on the east side. (An admission ticket is not required to enter the store on the east side of the Golden Ball.)

Next door, the double brick structure divided into the **Unicorn's Horn** and **John Carter's Store** was built in 1765 by two brothers. Dr. James Carter used the west portion as an apothecary shop under the distinctive sign of the unicorn's horn. His brother John ran a general store in the building's eastern half.

Across the street is ■**Wetherburn's Tavern,** one of the most important of the town's

surviving buildings because it has been so thoroughly documented—architecturally as a carefully studied original building, archaeologically through extensive excavations, and historically by surviving deeds, accounts, and a room-by-room inventory taken after the death of Henry Wetherburn, its long-time owner-operator, in 1760.

A colonial tavern was quite different from its modern namesake. In addition to serving spirits and ale, it also offered lodging for

Charlton House

■*Wetherburn's Tavern*

■*The Golden Ball*
(Silversmith)

Unicorn's Horn and
John Carter's Store

travelers, meals, and a place for socializing and entertaining. Cards, dice, and conversation were as important as food and drink. Wetherburn's "great room," which measures twenty-five feet square and occupies most of the west end of the first floor, occasionally served as an informal town hall in which scientific lectures, political gatherings, and balls took place.

A large-scale enterprise, Wetherburn's depended on the enslaved to cook, serve, clean, tend the garden, and groom customers' horses. Henry Wetherburn owned twelve slaves, including seven women (one with a young daughter), an adult man, and three boys. They would have lived in the attics over the kitchen and stable.

After Wetherburn's death in 1760, a long and detailed inventory of his estate listed the contents of the building room by room. It has been a principal guide in refurnishing the restored tavern. Additional information came from the painstaking excavations made by Colonial Williamsburg archaeologists who recovered more than two hundred thousand fragments of pottery, glass, and metal objects from the site.

The outbuildings, vegetable garden, and yard form one of the most thoroughly researched dependency areas in Williamsburg. The dairy survives with its original framing. The other outbuildings, including the kitchen in which there is a huge fireplace, were reconstructed on their eighteenth-century locations,

which were revealed by modern archaeological excavations.

In 1770, wigmaker Edward Charlton owned the neighboring **Charlton House**. Charlton kept an account book that details his wigmaking activities between 1769 and 1774. It shows that his customers included burgesses—such as Thomas Jefferson, Patrick Henry, and Colonel Lewis Burwell of Kingsmill plantation—and town residents—George Wythe, Thomas Everard, Peyton Randolph, and Peter Pelham to name a few—as well as local tavern keepers, merchants, and tradesmen. In addition to charges for wigs (brown

dress bob wigs at two pounds, three shillings, were popular), shaving, and hair dressing, Charlton also sold pairs of curls to the wives and daughters of his customers.

Williamsburg's working version of a wig shop, the ■**King's Arms Barber Shop**, has been reconstructed. Today, it carries on the

Tarpley's Store

services of wig making, barbering, and hair-dressing. In colonial days, a **wigmaker** was also known as a peruke-maker.

Jane Vobe, one of Williamsburg's most successful tavern keepers, ran the **King's Arms Tavern.** In 1772, she announced her location as "opposite the Raleigh, at the Sign of the King's Arms," a name that she changed to the Eagle Tavern after the Revolution.

During the war, when Mrs. Vobe supplied food and drink to American troops, Baron von Steuben ran up a bill of nearly three hundred Spanish dollars for lodging, meals, and beverages. Today, the King's Arms offers traditional southern dishes served in an atmosphere reminiscent of colonial days.

The reconstructed **Alexander Purdie House** serves as the east wing of the King's Arms Tavern. In 1774, the Scottish-born Purdie founded the third of three Williamsburg newspapers named the *Virginia Gazette.* All three papers competed for readers as the Revolution drew near.

The **John Coke Office** next door was named for an early-nineteenth-century keeper of the Raleigh Tavern.

Across the street is the ■**Raleigh Tavern,** the foremost of Williamsburg's taverns in the eighteenth century. Established about 1717, the Raleigh Tavern grew in size and reputation through the years. Letters, diaries, newspaper advertisements, and other records indicate that the Raleigh was one of the most important taverns in colonial Virginia. It served as

a center for social, commercial, and political gatherings; small private and large public dinners; lectures and exhibitions; and auctions of merchandise, land, and the enslaved.

During "Publick Times," when the high courts were in session, the Raleigh Tavern hummed with activity. Gentlemen and ladies attended elegant balls in its popular Apollo Room. Planters and merchants gathered at its bar. Sturdy tavern tables were scarred by dice boxes; tobacco smoke from long clay pipes filled the air. Good fellowship and business deals were sealed by a toast of Madeira or by a pint of ale drunk from a pewter tankard.

Although he generally stayed elsewhere, George Washington often noted in his diary that he "dined at the Raleigh." After one evening of revelry in 1763, twenty-year-old Thomas Jefferson, then reading law under the learned George Wythe's supervision, complained in a letter to a friend: "Last night as merry as agreeable company and dancing with Belinda in the Apollo could make me, I never could have thought the succeeding Sun would have seen me so wretched."

Public receptions were common. In 1775, Peyton Randolph was entertained at the Raleigh Tavern when he returned from serving as the president of the first Continental Congress, which met in Philadelphia. The following year, Virginia troops in Williamsburg gave a farewell dinner in honor of their esteemed commander, Patrick Henry. After the preliminary agreement on a treaty ending the Revolution

John Coke Office   Alexander Purdie House   King's Arms Tavern   ■ King's Arms Barber Shop (Wigmaker)

■ *Raleigh Tavern*

To *Raleigh Tavern Kitchen* and *Raleigh Tavern Bakery*

was proclaimed in the city, the citizens of the new republic concluded their triumphal parade with a celebration at the Raleigh Tavern. General Lafayette was welcomed on his return to Williamsburg in 1824 with a banquet in the Apollo Room.

The tavern's location, its convenient meeting rooms, and (one suspects) its proprietors' sympathies made it a center of political activity in the colonial capital during the 1760s and 1770s. In 1769, when royal governor Lord Botetourt dissolved the General Assembly

Becoming Americans
Our Struggle to Be Both Free and Equal

THE INSTITUTION OF SLAVERY

Slavery created great divisions in eighteenth-century Virginia because it fostered the development of a social structure based on race.

The rise of the plantation system and the dwindling supply of white servants led to the large-scale importation of slaves. Europeans forced the migration of twelve million Africans between the sixteenth and nineteenth centuries. Approximately six hundred thousand were brought into British North America.

A series of laws formalized Virginia's system of slavery. By the late seventeenth century, as the number of Africans in the colony was on the rise, legislators began passing laws to define who was a slave and to make slavery permanent and hereditary. When Virginia's slave population grew substantially after 1700, colonial leaders enacted more laws to restrict the movement of slaves, to set punishments for legal infractions, and to reinforce a slaveholder's right to his or her human property. As a result, the cultural, religious, and social differences between blacks and whites became sharper in the eighteenth century.

Although Africans could not alter formal institutions, individual slaves were able to shape personal relationships with whites. They also participated in a local, increasingly cash-based trading economy. Blacks and whites influenced one another's speech and culture as well. Rather than being a process that blacks or whites consciously pursued, cultural sharing was the inevitable result of their interaction in all areas of their lives.

because of its protest against the Townshend Acts, many indignant burgesses reconvened at the Raleigh to draw up a boycott of British goods. Five years later, the Assembly again being dissolved, other nonimportation measures were agreed upon at the Raleigh Tavern after the shocking news reached Virginia that Great Britain had ordered the port of Boston closed. The "late representatives of the people" issued the call for delegates from all the colonies to meet in the first Continental Congress.

The Raleigh Tavern burned in 1859. Architects who reconstructed the building were aided by two drawings made in 1848, by insurance policies, and by archaeological excavations that revealed most of the original foundations of the tavern and many colonial artifacts. Inventories of the possessions of its eighteenth-century proprietors guided the refurnishing of the Raleigh Tavern. After the death of Anthony Hay in 1770, for example, the inventory listed most articles in the tavern.

The gentlemen of colonial Virginia and their ladies would find little changed if they returned to dance their minuets again. Charter members of the Phi Beta Kappa Society,

Alexander Craig House   Scrivener Store

founded in Williamsburg in 1776, could once more meet in the Apollo Room. The Raleigh Tavern's pervasive spirit of hospitality is well expressed in the motto gilded over the Apollo Room mantel: *Hilaritas Sapientiae et Bonae Vitae Proles*—"Jollity, the offspring of wisdom and good living."

Today, guests can purchase bread, cookies, and other baked products at the **Raleigh Tavern Bakery** in the **Raleigh Tavern Kitchen.** (An admission ticket is not required to enter the Raleigh Tavern Bakery.)

Commercial establishments lined nearly all the rest of Duke of Gloucester Street from the Raleigh Tavern to the Capitol. The **Alexander Craig House, Scrivener Store, Nicolson Store,** and **John Crump House** were, respectively, a

The Apollo Room.

LOOKING NORTH

■ *Pasteur & Galt Apothecary Shop*

*Nicolson Store

John Crump House

Edinburgh Castle Tavern

saddle and harness shop, grocery store, general store, and residence.

At midcentury, **Edinburgh Castle Tavern** and **Shields Tavern** competed for the trade of the traveling public. In the early 1740s, James Shields took over the tavern that his Huguenot father-in-law, John Marot, had operated several decades earlier. Although located close to the Capitol, Shields Tavern attracted lower gentry and successful middling customers. Present-day guests will find a setting in the style of an eighteenth-century coffeehouse. From 1772 to 1795, the building was the residence of Dr. John de Sequeyra, eighteenth-century Williamsburg's only known resident of Jewish descent.

At the ■**Pasteur & Galt Apothecary Shop,** Dr. William Pasteur and Dr. John Galt had a partnership from 1775 to 1778. Both of these apothecary-surgeons apprenticed in Williamsburg and studied at Saint Thomas's Hospital in London. Today, the shop displays copies of Dr. Galt's certificates in surgery and anatomy, midwifery, and the theory of

medicine from London. Antique English and Dutch jars, pharmaceutical equipment, a traveling medical kit, and surgical tools, some original to the site, are also on display.

The shop also features reproduction splints for broken bones and dental tools for cleaning and extracting teeth. Period medications such as tincture of Peruvian bark for intermittent fever, chalk troches for heartburn, and licorce root for sore throat are also featured, as are

Shields Tavern

LOOKING SOUTH

other preparations containing active ingredients used in medicine today.

The building nearest the Capitol on the south side of Duke of Gloucester Street is the **Palmer House,** which bears the name of John Palmer, lawyer and bursar of the College of William and Mary. Palmer built his house on the site of an old store. During the Civil War, the dwelling served as a military headquarters, first for Confederate General Joseph Johnston and then for General George B. McClellan, the commander of the Union forces. The holes in the brickwork, known as putlog holes, were left when the masons who built the Palmer House removed their scaffolding.

Merchants met in the open area that terminates Duke of Gloucester Street just before the Capitol wall to set prices of tobacco and other agricultural products and to trade in commercial paper. The Exchange functioned much like a modern commodities market, dealing in futures and risk. After the capital moved to Richmond in 1780, the Exchange—like Williamsburg as a whole—decreased in importance.

In October 1765, the Exchange was the scene of a near-riot when Colonel George Mercer, distributor of stamps for Virginia, arrived in Williamsburg from London prepared to distribute stamped paper when the hated Stamp Act went into effect on November 1. A large group of merchants and planters surrounded Mercer as he attempted to reach Governor Fauquier who was waiting with other high-ranking government officials on the porch of a nearby coffeehouse. The crowd demanded to know if Mercer intended to resign. He replied that he would answer them

MEET . . . ROBERT NICOLSON

"We intend to make use of a House in the City of Williamsburgh . . . as a place of Public Worship of God according to the Practise of Protestant Dissenters of the Presbyterian denomination." So stated Robert Nicolson of Williamsburg and sixteen other men in a petition to a local court in 1765. Notifying the court enabled them to worship legally outside the Church of England in Virginia.

Before he became a dissenter, Nicolson and his wife, Mary, probably walked to Bruton Parish Church to worship on Sundays. They paid taxes that the vestry levied to meet church expenses, which included the minister's salary and support for the poor. If Robert and Mary missed too many services, Anglican churchwardens could take them to court, a good reason to attend church regularly.

Although he had become a Presbyterian, Robert Nicolson still was obliged to pay taxes to support Bruton Parish Church. Nicolson's decision to proclaim himself a dissenter made him one of a growing number of Virginians who wanted the freedom to worship as they chose.

A tailor by trade, Nicolson also took in lodgers and kept a store. Over time he acquired a lot in town, thirty-five acres in the country, and two slaves, but Nicolson never rose above the middling rank of Williamsburg society.

In 1776, the General Assembly suspended the requirement that dissenters pay parish taxes. The legislature passed the Virginia Statute for Religious Freedom ten years later.

on November 1, after he had met with the governor.

The angry men followed Mercer to the coffeehouse where he joined Fauquier. The crowd demanded an answer before the act went into effect and began to storm the porch. Fauquier and other officials stepped forward to shield Mercer. The forward push stopped. Mercer reluctantly agreed to give an answer before November 1, and the governor escorted him to the Palace. Mercer resigned the next day.

The House of Burgesses had passed protest resolves introduced by Patrick Henry and supported by his famous Caesar-Brutus speech in May 1765. Virginians continued to argue strongly that the Stamp Act was an abridgement of their traditional British liberties because a legislature (Parliament) in which they were not represented had enacted it.

Palmer House

LOOKING NORTH

NICHOLSON STREET

*Public Gaol

*Secretary's Office

X

Tickets, Treasures, and Books

Powell's Tenement

The Blue Bell

D
R C

Capitol

DUKE OF GLOUCESTER STREET

BLAIR STREET

WALLER STREET

Presbyterian Meetinghouse

Ayscough House
(Gunsmith)

FRANCIS STREET

SECTION

3

The Capitol
and Its
Surroundings

Section 3
Admission Ticket Required
Places to Shop
Other Places to Visit
Exhibition Gardens
Places to Dine
Lodging
Services or Privately Occupied

R Restrooms
C Public Telephones
D Cold Drinks
▲ Water Fountains
X Buy Tickets Here
* Original Building
♿ Accessible to Those with Disabilities

0   100   200   300   400   500 FEET

LOOKING NORTH

■ *Capitol*

THE CAPITOL AND ITS SURROUNDINGS

An asterisk indicates that a building is an original eighteenth- or nineteenth-century structure. A blue box indicates that you need an admission ticket to see an attraction.

For eighty years, Williamsburg was the political center of Virginia, one of England's largest, wealthiest, and most populous colonies. Here laws and justice were made and administered on behalf of all colonial Virginians. The first and second Capitol buildings, the Public Gaol, and the Secretary's Office were visible reminders that these buildings and the activities that went on inside them gave Williamsburg a political importance second to that of no other colonial capital.

At the Capitol, the General Assembly debated and framed legislation and high court judges ruled on the most serious cases and dispensed justice. Most of the important records of the colony—legal documents of every kind—were kept in a separate building, the Secretary's Office. Nearby, at the Public Gaol, Virginians accused of felonies or imprisoned for debts languished until their cases could be heard in court.

Spring and fall sessions of the General Court, summer and winter sessions of the criminal court, and sessions of the General Assembly, which were convened by the governor, provided the formal occasions that brought the Capitol area to life. Other, more informal activities animated the scene year-round because the bureaucratic machinery that kept the wheels of government turning operated day in and day out.

The H-shaped plan of the ■Capitol reflects the division of the government between the lower and upper houses of the legislature.

Representative government in Virginia began at Jamestown in 1619. As the General Assembly evolved, it comprised the Council and the House of Burgesses, each of which met separately.

The east wing of the Capitol contained the House of Burgesses on the first floor and committee rooms for the burgesses on the second. The House of Burgesses, the lower house of the legislature, consisted of two members elected by the landowners of each county and one member each from Jamestown, Williamsburg, Norfolk, and the College of William and Mary.

The west wing housed the General Courtroom on the first floor and the Council

Chamber on the second. The Council, made up of twelve leading colonists appointed for life by the king, constituted the upper house of the legislature. The councillors also assisted the governor by acting as a council of state. In its legislative capacity, the Council met in the elegant Council Chamber. Each wing had its own staircase.

The General Assembly convened periodically in the Capitol to act on a wide range of legislation. In the course of a session, which could have lasted a few days or several weeks, the upper and lower houses might have considered the petition of a veteran for public assistance or frontier settlers asking that a new county or church parish be formed. The legislators could divide large counties into smaller ones or move a county's courthouse to a more central location. They considered aiding other colonies in wartime and at the same time established Virginia's own frontier defenses. They settled public claims and levied

Plan of the ground floor of the reconstructed Capitol

Plan of the upper floor of the reconstructed Capitol

taxes to pay for them. And, as the imperial crisis of the 1760s and 1770s worsened, they spent more and more time debating remonstrations to submit to King George III and Parliament.

If the two houses deadlocked in trying to pass a bill already accepted by one or the other, representatives from the Council and the burgesses met jointly in the second-floor chamber located over the piazza. In effect, this conference room formed a bridge between the two buildings. The architecture of the Capitol thus aided the process of mediation between the two houses. Morning prayers were also held in the conference room.

The foundations of the original building were laid in 1701. Impatient with meeting at the College of William and Mary, Virginia's lawmakers moved into the new Capitol in 1704, a year before its completion.

As a precaution against fire, Williamsburg's first Capitol was designed without chimneys, and the use of fire, candles, or tobacco was strictly prohibited. In time, such safeguards were sacrificed to necessity and convenience. A secretary complained, for example, that his records were "exposed by the Damps." Two chimneys were therefore added in 1723. Despite precautions, however, fire gutted the building on January 30, 1747, leaving "the naked Brick Walls only . . . standing."

Governor William Gooch helped defeat a proposal to move the government further to the west after the fire. Thus, a second Capitol, completed in 1753, was built in Williamsburg. It incorporated the surviving walls of its predecessor but differed in appearance. After the removal of Virginia's government to Richmond in 1780, the second building fell into disrepair, and, in 1832, it too was destroyed by fire.

Before reconstruction could be undertaken, Colonial Williamsburg faced a dilemma: should the first or second building rise again on the old foundations? The second Capitol

was of greater historic interest, since it witnessed the events of the years before the Revolution, but the first Capitol could lay claim to greater architectural distinction. Its rounded ends, for instance, were unique. Moreover, long searching of the architectural evidence disclosed voluminous information about the earlier building, whereas few records were available for the later one. As a result, the first Capitol was reconstructed.

Two courts met regularly in the Capitol. The General Court, the highest court in the colony, convened in April and October to hear both civil and criminal cases. The governor and the twelve members of the Council served as the justices of the General Court. After 1710, the Court of Oyer and Terminer (meaning "to hear and decide"), presided over by the councillors alone, heard criminal cases at sessions in June and December.

Punishment for serious crimes was harsh in the eighteenth century, and the death penalty was the rule for offenses such as arson, horse stealing, forgery, burglary—and piracy. First offenders or criminals with particularly moving pleas might, however, receive clemency. In 1727, convicted teenage pirate John Vidal, who pitifully protested that he "never

The Union flag (left) *became the national standard of Great Britain and her colonies in 1606. The Great Union flag* (right) *became the first American flag to fly in Williamsburg on May 15, 1776.*

Historic furnishings help convey the atmosphere of formality that existed in the Capitol. The Speaker's chair in the House of Burgesses was probably made by a Williamsburg cabinetmaker in the 1730s for the first Capitol. Moved to Richmond with the state's possessions in 1780, this imposing piece returned to Williamsburg through the courtesy of the Virginia legislature.

intended to go a-pirating" and "with a weeping heart" begged for mercy, received His Majesty's most gracious pardon.

Ceremony and formality characterized the proceedings of these legislative and judicial bodies and the behavior of their members. When a new governor arrived, he was customarily met by a delegation and conveyed directly to the Capitol to be sworn to the king's commission. The opening ceremony of the General Assembly was patterned after the opening of Parliament. Lord Botetourt rode down Duke of Gloucester Street to the Capitol in a gilded state coach drawn by six matching gray horses. Burgesses assembled in the Council Chamber, took their oaths of office in the presence of the Council, and returned to the House to elect a Speaker. On the governor's formal approval of the Speaker's election, the mace of the House, which had been placed under the table, was returned to the tabletop and the burgesses proceeded with their legislative business.

Parliamentary privilege exercised by the English parliament extended to the House of Burgesses to protect the House and its members against slander. In 1723, burgess Mathew Kemp complained that attorney William Hopkins had uttered "several rude Contemptious and undecent Expressions" about Kemp's conduct in the House. The burgesses found Hopkins guilty of contempt and ordered him to kneel, "acknowlege his Offence, and ask pardon of this House and Mr. Kemp." Hopkins refused. The burgesses next ordered that Hopkins, wearing a sign that proclaimed his offenses, be led from the Capitol to the college and back again. Then he was to be imprisoned. On hearing this, a chastened Hopkins knelt, expressed sorrow, and prayed mercy of the House, which fined and then discharged him.

Some of the colony's most powerful officials had offices in the Capitol. The secretary, usually a member of the Council, was appointed by the king. His office issued all land patents and most other documents, including naturalization papers and passports, that required the seal of the colony.

The auditor examined all colonial revenue accounts and forwarded them to Treasury officials in London. The receiver general took in and disbursed the colony's "royal revenues." The attorney general also had an office in the Capitol. He gave legal advice to the governor and his Council, prosecuted criminal cases before the General Court, and, after 1720, served as the sole judge of the Vice Admiralty Court. Because he was the king's attorney, the attorney general was never a councillor.

A memorable historical event occurred at the Capitol on May 15, 1776, when Virginia's legislators pledged their lives and fortunes by taking the daring step of declaring their full freedom from England. Without a dissenting vote, the burgesses adopted a resolution

Becoming Americans
Our Struggle to Be Both Free and Equal

CHOOSING REVOLUTION

Colonial Williamsburg's programs trace the development of the new nation by exploring the complex decision every Virginian faced: whether to remain loyal to the British Crown or to separate from the mother country.

When Virginia's political leaders began to protest imperial policies in the early 1760s, none imagined a separate nation. Yet by the middle of the next decade, issues and choices had transformed traditional ideals of British liberty into a revolutionary American political philosophy based on freedom, liberty, and popular sovereignty that Americans were ready to defend with arms.

Two contending groups were central to the conflict between Virginia and Great Britain. After the Seven Years' War, the British ministry, backed by Parliament, sought active management of the vast empire that Britain had acquired. Their policies often came into conflict with Virginia's powerful political leaders who were determined to protect their prerogative to draft legislation for the colony.

Political leaders in Virginia were generally united on the basic issues, but they divided over the best course to follow. The elder statesmen tended to be conservative. They counseled moderation. The younger, more aggressive leadership urged forceful and direct protests against British policies that threatened property rights. To protest effectively, they needed the support of the yeomanry. Increasingly diverse in ethnicity and religion, the yeomanry responded to the gentry leadership's appeal to property rights by becoming active politically. The gentry's promotion of property ownership as almost a sacred right protected the practice of slavery, however.

Going to war against Great Britain was a bold—some said a suicidal—act. Once war was declared, whites of all social ranks, free blacks, the enslaved, and Native Americans considered both ideology and self-interest as they chose, or did not choose, revolution. Taking one side or the other required sacrifice. A significant number sat on the fence as long as possible. Some switched sides. Dependent family members usually accepted the choice of the head of the household and shared in the consequences, although sons or slaves occasionally made opposite choices.

Out of the war came American principles of nation building, among them the conflicting ideals of individual liberty and the public good. Through government channels established by the U.S. Constitution, Americans today continue to struggle to achieve a balance between these two ideals and to extend them to groups that have not enjoyed them. Americans ceaselessly reexamine how to attain liberty, freedom, and equality, the ideals for which the American Revolution was fought.

Secretary's Office

instructing Virginia's delegation in Philadelphia to propose American independence.

On June 7, 1776, Richard Henry Lee, one of Virginia's delegates, acting on this resolution, introduced a motion for independence on the floor of the Continental Congress at Philadelphia. His proposal led directly to the Declaration of Independence, drafted largely by Thomas Jefferson, who had stood at the half-open door of the House of Burgesses in Williamsburg eleven years before to hear

Patrick Henry, the first governor of the Commonwealth of Virginia.

Patrick Henry thunder his defiance of Parliament and king.

Before a separate Secretary's Office was built, the most important public papers of the colony were stored in an office next to the General Courtroom. There, the chief clerk and

his deputy oversaw a vast domain of records in the form of bound volumes and of endless files of loose papers tied up in red tape that had been used by bureaucrats to secure legal and official documents since the seventeenth century. Here, generations of clerk-apprentices scribbled away, learning their trade.

When the Capitol burned in 1747, officials fortunately were able to save a number of documents that included land office records, executive papers of the clerk of the Council, and the files of the clerk of the House of Burgesses. Afterward, it took nearly a year to sort them all out.

After the fire, the burgesses and Council agreed in principle on the necessity of building a separate **Secretary's Office.** But while the burgesses' approval was delayed by a debate about whether to move the capital farther inland, the Council acted decisively. It contracted for and oversaw the erection of a repository for the public records. The building was completed at a cost of nearly four hundred pounds, paid for out of royal revenues, by December 1748.

The new Secretary's Office was clearly designed to avoid fire at all costs. There was neither basement nor attic, the original floor was paved with stones, and the interior walls and window jambs were plastered-over brick. Little wood was used in the construction. There were, however, four fireplaces in the three-room structure to provide heat in winter

*Public Gaol

and drive off the damp and mold in summer. Tidewater humidity can be as destructive as fire to paper and leather.

It would be hard to overestimate the potential influence in the colony of the office of the secretary. Perhaps the most significant of his privileges was the power to appoint the clerks of all the county courts in Virginia. To supply a trained cadre of these young men, five to seven apprentice clerks were always at work in the Secretary's Office. Sent there to serve an apprenticeship of seven years, they then waited their turn to be named to the next vacant clerkship. This system produced a body of clerks who had been trained to the same standards.

After the capital and its records moved to Richmond in 1780, the Secretary's Office was occupied for a time by the Court of Admiralty under Justice Benjamin Waller. When the Capitol became a private grammar school, the Secretary's Office was refitted as a home for the headmaster. Today, it houses a gift shop where you can purchase books, gift items, and admission tickets.

The ■**Public Gaol** (pronounced "jail"), just north of the Capitol on Nicholson Street, affords today grim evidence of crime and punishment in colonial America.

Accused offenders were imprisoned in the Gaol only until their cases came to trial in the Capitol before either the General Court or the Court of Oyer and Terminer. Insolvent debtors awaiting relief or mercy were occasionally held in the Gaol. Their numbers were greatly reduced by a 1772 act that made creditors wholly responsible for their debtors' maintenance and tripled the fees charged for their board. Runaway slaves were detained at the Gaol until their masters claimed them and paid their expenses.

The Gaol at times housed insane people and military prisoners. Until the Public Hospital opened in 1773, some mentally ill individuals were occasionally confined in the Gaol. In the early years of the Revolution, the Gaol was crowded with captured British redcoats, Tory sympathizers, and accused traitors, deserters, and spies. Henry Hamilton, the British governor of the Northwest Territory, widely known as the "Hair Buyer" because he allegedly paid his Indian allies for American scalps, was detained in the Public Gaol in 1779–1780.

Prison conditions in colonial days would be judged both crude and cruel by modern standards. The use of leg irons, handcuffs, and chains seems inhumane. Even if the night was bitterly cold, prisoners of every description bedded down with only a thin blanket. A diet of "salt beef damaged, and Indian meal" could not have been very appetizing. Yet prisoners were allowed to converse and walk about the exercise yard during the day, to use the crude sanitary arrangements (the "thrones" in each cell), and to take "physick,"

MEET . . . PETER PELHAM

Peter Pelham was a man of much ability. Born in England in 1721, Pelham came to America in 1726 with his father. They settled in Boston where Pelham studied music and became organist at Trinity Church. Pelham became artist John Singleton Copley's stepbrother when his father married Copley's widowed mother.

Pelham moved to Williamsburg about 1750. In 1755, he not only set up the new organ ordered for Bruton Parish Church but also was "unanimously appointed and chosen organist." As a member of the Williamsburg Lodge of Masons, Pelham played the organ at the funeral of fellow Mason and *Virginia Gazette* publisher William Rind. Pelham taught young ladies to play the harpsichord and spinet, and he served as musical director when *The Beggar's Opera* was first performed in Williamsburg.

Pelham and his wife, Ann, had fourteen children, some of whom died in infancy. Like many artists then and now, Pelham's musical talents did not always generate enough income to maintain his large family. He supplemented his income by serving as clerk to governors Fauquier and Botetourt and as keeper of the Public Gaol. Until he left Williamsburg in 1802, "the modern Orpheus—the inimitable Pelham" continued as church organist, and he also gave weekly concerts to the delight of many townsfolk.

---

or medicine, when ill. Prisoners with money or accommodating friends could purchase food and liquor from one of the taverns nearby or obtain clothing and blankets to supplement those issued at the Gaol.

Legislation that was passed in 1701 called for the construction of a "substantial Brick Prison" twenty by thirty feet. The act further provided for an adjoining walled exercise yard. Debtors' cells were added in 1711, and quarters for the gaoler were built in 1722. In its present form, the Public Gaol has three rooms on the first floor—a hall and chamber for the gaoler and his family and a cell at the rear for debtors—and "chambers" in the attic for the gaoler's use

and the confinement of prisoners.

The gaolkeepers, who often served as custodians of the Capitol, were appointed by the governor. Gaolers had a rough and dangerous job for which they were paid a modest salary.

The first keeper, John Redwood, received thirty pounds annually. This amount was supplemented by prisoners' fees and eventually increased by the General Assembly.

The Gaol served colony and commonwealth until 1780. A portion of the original building continued to be used by the city of Williamsburg as its jail until 1910. Part of the brickwork of the Gaol's massive walls is original. Shackles unearthed in the course of the building's restoration are evidence of the

Ayscough House (Gunsmith)

bleak life of a colonial criminal.

The ■**Ayscough House** was the site of one of many establishments that grew up around the Capitol. Artisans, retailers, and tavern keepers located near the Capitol enjoyed the business of the councillors, burgesses, attorneys, and others who came to participate in court cases or deliberate legislation. Proximity to the Capitol did not ensure success, however. Christopher Ayscough, a former gardener, and his wife, Anne, who had been the head cook for Lieutenant Governor Francis Fauquier at the Palace, purchased the Ayscough House and established a tavern there in 1768. The funds probably came from a bequest of 250 pounds that Governor Fauquier left Anne "in recompense of her great fidelity and attention to me in all my illnesses and of the great Economy with which she conducted the Expenses of my Kitchen during my residence at Williamsburg."

The Ayscoughs' tavern-keeping venture proved to be short-lived, however. Within two years, Christopher Ayscough, deeply in debt, offered to sell his dwelling along with furnishings, Madeira wine, slaves, and horses. Ayscough then became the doorkeeper at the Capitol, but, in 1771, he was discharged for drunkenness. Today, **gunsmiths** at the Ayscough House use the tools and methods of their predecessors to make rifles, fowling pieces, and pistols like those crafted in colonial Virginia.

Powell's Tenement   *The Blue Bell*

In 1703, John Redwood, keeper of the Public Gaol, obtained a lot east of the Capitol where he operated an ordinary. At various times in the eighteenth century, **The Blue Bell** housed a tavern, a lodging house, a store, a gunsmith's shop, and a tenement. After being informed in 1771 that his Williamsburg property, including the Blue Bell, was in "bad repair always rented to bad tenants, always nasty and few rents paid," absentee owner William Lee of London tried to sell the tavern but failed to find a buyer.

Wheelwright and riding chair maker Peter Powell rented a shop on the site of **Powell's Tenement** from 1755 to about 1770. In 1766, Powell advertised for an assistant, a blacksmith "who understands doing riding chair work." Later, in 1779, Powell's Tenement was occupied by the keeper of the Public Gaol.

The reconstructed building now houses the heating plant for the Capitol. **Powell's Kitchen** is behind.

In 1934, the year the reconstructed Capitol opened, John D. Rockefeller Jr. addressed a commemorative session of the Virginia General Assembly. This was the first of many times that the Virginia legislature has met in the Capitol in Colonial Williamsburg's Historic Area.

MEET . . . THOMAS WALKER

On March 6, 1750, Dr. Thomas Walker and five companions set out on a journey from Albemarle County. They traveled beyond the southwesternmost settlement in Virginia and through the Cumberland Gap into Kentucky before returning more than four months later. Dr. Walker and his colleagues were not the first whites to reach Kentucky, but, unlike earlier explorers, Walker kept careful notes of where he went and what he saw because the trip was more than an exciting adventure. As the general agent of the Loyal Land Company, Walker was expected to locate the best possible eight hundred thousand acres granted to the company in July 1749.

Thomas Walker was born into a prominent family in King and Queen County in 1715. He moved to Williamsburg to live with his sister Mary and her husband, Dr. George Gilmer, as a teenager. Walker studied medicine in the colonial capital and then established a practice in Fredericksburg. Dr. Walker married Mildred, the widow of Nicholas Meriwether, in 1741. Managing his wife's dower lands at the foot of the Blue Ridge Mountains led to a new career for Walker. He began a long association with men such as Peter Jefferson and Joshua Fry who saw Virginia's and their own futures tied to western expansion. Walker devoted his considerable skills to merging the interests of the Loyal Land Company, which he helped to create, with his own until his death.

Elected a burgess in 1752, Walker served regularly until 1775. Putting his knowledge of the West to good use, he lobbied effectively to protect the company from rivals. Walker entertained Indian delegations on their way to Williamsburg at his Albemarle home, and the trust he gained among them earned him successive appointments as a chief Indian negotiator. In that position, he was as attentive to Loyal Land Company interests as he was to Virginia's.

When Thomas Walker died in 1794, the Loyal Land Company had sold more than two hundred thousand acres in more than nine hundred tracts. What once had been Virginia's southwest frontier had become home to thirty-eight thousand settlers. And Kentucky was a new state in a new, westward-looking nation.

In 1755, Virginia was much larger than it is today.

LOOKING NORTH

Governor's Palace

D Robert Carter Office

C

*Robert Carter House

McKenzie Shop

PALACE STREET

PALACE GREEN

PALACE STREET

D R ▲

Thomas Everard
*House and Office

▲

Play Booth
Theater

Levingston
Kitchen

Elkanah Deane
House

Elkanah Deane
Shop

PRINCE GEORGE ST.

▲

Weaver

Basketmaker

*George Wythe House

NICHOLSON
STREET

*Bruton Parish
Church

DUKE OF GLOUCESTER
STREET

SECTION

4

Around Palace Green

☐ Section 4	R	Restrooms
☐ Admission Ticket Required	C	Public Telephones
☐ Places to Shop	D	Cold Drinks
■ Other Places to Visit	▲	Water Fountains
☐ Exhibition Gardens	X	Buy Tickets Here
☐ Places to Dine	*	Original Building
☐ Lodging	♿	Accessible to Those with Disabilities
☐ Services or Privately Occupied		

0   100   200   300   400   500 FEET

AROUND PALACE GREEN

An asterisk indicates that a building is an original eighteenth- or nineteenth-century structure. A blue box indicates that you need an admission ticket to see an attraction.

When eighteenth-century visitors turned north from Duke of Gloucester Street onto Palace Street, they looked down a long expanse of open ground that terminated at the Governor's Palace. One contemporary described the vista: "Toward the center of the city . . . is the Governor's Palace, very well built, very spacious, with a big lawn . . . which forms a pretty avenue." Rows of catalpa trees planted one hundred feet apart flanked the green.

The spacious homes built here after mid-century had a formal appearance favored by their gentry owners. In the eighteenth century, however, Palace Street was not entirely residential.

From the 1730s on, unsightly piles of coal used to fuel the Geddy forge and foundry were in full view in the backyard of the James Geddy House on the corner of Palace and Duke of Gloucester Streets. In the 1760s, a lead manufactory was in operation beyond the Wythe property; by the 1770s, a busy carriage-building shop was located behind the Elkanah Deane House. In the eighteenth century, polite society had not yet chosen to remove itself completely from the presence of the workaday world, and mixed residential neighborhoods like that around Palace Green were common.

Behind the houses on Palace Green, as elsewhere in Williamsburg, lived and worked the town's slaves. Signs of their presence—the currycombs of the grooms, the pots and pans

of the cooks, and the pails of the housemaids—could be found all around these work areas. By the time of the Revolution, fully half the town's population was black.

Here and there, tucked into corners or hidden in lofts above kitchens, stables, and other outbuildings, were the slaves' scant personal possessions: a straw-filled mattress, one or two extra pieces of clothing, an occasional fiddle or banjo. These few material goods only begin to suggest the full cultural life that Africans and their descendants created in the New World. In Williamsburg's backyards, black men and women courted, married, and reared children. They told African folk tales adapted to life in Virginia, taught their children how to cope with the harsh realities of slavery, and attempted to subvert the system by harboring runaway slaves.

William Levingston bought three lots at the corner of Palace and Nicholson Streets in 1716. Soon afterward, he built a house, kitchen, and other outbuildings. He also constructed a playhouse and laid out a bowling green. Today, the reconstructed **Levingston Kitchen** is all that remains on the site.

Levingston briefly operated a tavern at his house next door. He soon encountered financial difficulties and had to mortgage the property. The building continued to be used periodically. In 1736, "the young Gentlemen of the college" performed *The Tragedy of Cato*. Other plays were also presented.

This location changed in appearance and

*Thomas Everard House   Thomas Everard Office

character through the years. By the mid-1730s, Dr. George Gilmer, a successful apothecary-surgeon, had acquired the property, moved into the house, and built an apothecary shop on the corner.

The open-air ■ **Play Booth Theater** is located on the site of the first theater, which was active in the 1720s and 1730s. Archaeologists have unearthed the foundations of Levingston's playhouse. It measured eighty-six and a half feet long by thirty feet wide and stood at least two stories high, about the same size as English provincial theaters of the period. In 1718, to celebrate the birthday of King George I, Governor Spotswood sponsored the first play known to have been staged at the theater.

In 1745, Dr. Gilmer sold the theater to a group of subscribers who gave it to the city to be remodeled for a courthouse. The Hustings Court (Williamsburg's municipal court) met here until the city and James City County joined in erecting the brick Courthouse on Market Square in 1770. About the same time, the old playhouse was demolished.

The Play Booth Theater is similar to theaters erected for fairs and race days in England. Although performances sometimes attracted a boisterous, rowdy audience, the gentry also frequented playhouses—Thomas Jefferson and George Washington attended plays in Williamsburg. Today, actors at the Play Booth Theater present scenes from plays popular in Williamsburg before the American Revolution.

In 1788, St. George Tucker bought the house that Levingston had built. He moved it to a more desirable location fronting on Market Square, which had, since the 1750s, become an increasingly important focus of town life. (See the St. George Tucker House, a description of which begins on page 47.)

John Brush, gunsmith, armorer, and first keeper of the Magazine on Market Square, built the ■ **Thomas Everard House** in 1718. After Brush died in 1726, it had several different owners.

Dancing master and painter William Dering bought the house in 1742. Although he was not a member of the gentry himself, Dering associated with the upper classes. By the mid-eighteenth century, planters were turning to dancing masters because they wanted their children to learn the elaborate manners that an increasingly fashion-conscious society valued. The ability to dance a minuet in the Governor's Palace or the Apollo Room at the Raleigh Tavern meant that a person was a cultured member of polite society.

Thomas Everard arrived in Virginia as an orphan apprentice in the 1730s. Later a respected and wealthy local leader, Everard acquired the property about 1755 and lived there for twenty-five years. He was the clerk of the York County Court for nearly forty years, twice served as mayor of Williamsburg—in 1766 and 1771—and was on the vestry of Bruton Parish Church. Everard served as deputy clerk of the General Court from the 1740s until the Revolution.

The Thomas Everard House as originally constructed was a timber-framed one-and-a-half-story building typical of the houses built here in the early years of the eighteenth

Levingston Kitchen

century. It was covered with weatherboards that were prepared by hand-splitting four-foot lengths of oak boards. The roof was covered with clapboards instead of shingles. A section of the original roofing is still in place, protected over the centuries by the roof ridge of the north addition.

The house was later enlarged and embellished to reflect the standing of its owner and the changing taste by which a gentleman was judged. The addition of two wings at the back resulted in a U-shaped plan. Fine paneling and rich carving are evidence of Everard's affluence and taste.

The yard between the house and the outbuildings is paved with the original bricks discovered during the course of archaeological excavations. The wooden smokehouse and the brick kitchen are original buildings that have been restored. Everard's nineteen slaves lived and worked in these outbuildings. Today, an exhibition in the house focuses on Everard, his children, and his slaves.

■**Governor's Palace.** A description of the site begins on page 87.

The **Robert Carter House** on the west side of Palace Street was constructed by 1746. It served as Governor Dinwiddie's residence while the Palace underwent repairs in 1751 and 1752.

The first known owner was Charles Carter, son of Robert "King" Carter, one of the wealthiest Virginians in the colony. Robert Carter Nicholas, "King" Carter's grandson, purchased it in 1753. Long a leader of the House of Burgesses and treasurer of the colony, Nicholas made the house his home until

1761 when he sold it to Councillor Robert Carter, his cousin.

Robert Carter and his family lived in the house for twelve years. Six of his seventeen children were born here. Finding the dwelling "not sufficiently roomy," the Carter family returned to their plantation, called Nomini Hall, in 1772.

The house and the brick outbuilding are original. Other structures—including the unusual "breezeway"—are reconstructions. The Robert Carter Kitchen is now one of several Colonial Williamsburg hotel facilities in the Historic Area.

At midcentury, Dr. Kenneth McKenzie owned and lived on this property with his family. He operated his shop, **McKenzie Shop,** on the site. Dr. McKenzie died in 1755. Among other bequests, he left a sleleton to his "good friend Doctor James Carter having behaved in a very kind manner to me in my Sickness." Beverages, snacks, and ice cream are available for guests today.

The **Elkanah Deane House** was named for the Irish coachmaker who paid seven hundred pounds for four lots and the original dwelling, shop, and garden on this site in 1772. Deane may have been encouraged to move to Williamsburg from New York by royal governor Lord Dunmore. Deane advertised in the *Virginia Gazette* that he "had the Honour of making a Coach, Phaeton, and Chaise, for his Excellency the Right Honourable the Earle of Dunmore."

The same issue of the newspaper carried

MEET . . . BRISTOL

Callers at the front door of Thomas Everard's house were greeted by Bristol, Everard's black footman, who was dressed in livery. Bristol's uniform, a respectable suit trimmed with braid and brass buttons, was not as elegant as the livery worn by footmen at the Governor's Palace, however.

Everard had purchased Bristol, who was in his late twenties, from the estate of Governor Fauquier in 1768. The previous year Bristol had been baptized at Bruton Parish Church. The record of Bristol's baptism noted that he was a "new" slave, which indicates that he had recently arrived in Virginia, probably from the west coast of Africa. Everard owned other slaves—an elderly groom, two young men who waited on the table and did other chores, a cook, a laundress, and a housemaid.

As Everard's manservant, Bristol's main duty was to wait on his master. In the morning, he shaved him and laid out his clothes. At mealtimes, he supervised the young men who brought food to the table and served it. When Everard went out during the day, Bristol usually accompanied him. In the evening, he turned down his master's bed, used a bed warmer to take the chill off the sheets, and saw that the fire was well banked for the night.

Bristol was intelligent. He knew how to read (though could not write), so Everard relied on him to deliver messages, run errands, and purchase household provisions. Bristol was proud of his abilities and of the confidence his master placed in him, but he never forgot that he was a slave.

Bristol looked forward to running errands to the Governor's Palace. When he delivered his master's gift of fish and peaches to the governor, the butler tipped him generously. More importantly, Bristol's trips to the Palace often gave him the opportunity to visit with Venus, Everard's laundress who had been hired out to Lord Botetourt; Hannah, who was part of the Palace staff during Fauquier's and Botetourt's tenures in office; and other slaves who worked there.

McKenzie Shop

an advertisement from Joseph Beck, a stay-maker in New York City. Beck encouraged the "Ladies of Virginia" to give their orders for stays to Mrs. Deane who would "take their Measures" and forward them to New York. Beck promised satisfaction.

Tree box topiary and small-leaved lindens are features of the Elkanah Deane House garden.

Behind the Elkanah Deane House on Prince George Street is the ■Elkanah Deane Shop. In the eighteenth century, the shop was the scene of carriage making on a considerable scale. Wheelwrights, blacksmiths, and harnessmakers were among the artisans who worked together to make carts, wagons, riding chairs, and carriages. Today, Historic Trades **carpenters** use the shop seasonally as a joiner's workshop.

George Wythe, one of the most influential Americans of his era, lived in the brick ■**George Wythe House** on the west side of Palace Street. His father-in-law, Colonel Richard Taliaferro, is believed to have designed the house. In his will, Taliaferro gave George and Elizabeth Wythe use of the property for life. Wythe lived in the house from about 1755, around the time he married Elizabeth Taliaferro, until 1791, when he moved to Richmond to serve as a judge on Virginia's Court of Chancery.

The Wythe House served as headquarters for George Washington just before the siege of Yorktown. Rochambeau occupied it for several months while French troops were stationed in Williamsburg after Cornwallis's surrender in 1781.

Perhaps one of the grandest and most impressive private dwellings in town, the Wythe House represented the aspirations of the Virginia gentry during the second half of the eighteenth century. The plan of the house consists of four rooms on each of two full stories, with both floors centrally divided by a large stair passage. Two great chimneys rise between the paired rooms, thus affording a fireplace in all eight. The smaller windows in the second story have the same number of panes, or "lights," as those on the first floor, a device that increases the apparent size of the house. The exterior exhibits some of the best masonry work in town, featuring Flemish bond brickwork enframed with rubbed jambs, corners, and water table and gauged-brick belt course and splayed brick arches.

Although little is known about the specific personal property of George and Elizabeth Wythe, the house has been furnished with objects typically found in comparable Virginia gentry homes. Architectural and documentary evidence suggests that this dwelling was once wallpapered virtually throughout. The yellow ocher trim color, discovered through recent paint analysis, complements the brightly colored wallpaper exhibited in the house. A comprehensive study of wallpaper usage in colonial Virginia provided the documentation for the wide variety of patterns and colors used throughout the building.

Behind the house, a symmetrical garden

Robert Carter House   *Robert Carter Office*

*George Wythe House

plan divides the property into distinct areas. Archaeological excavations established the locations of major outbuildings in the service yard, which is adjacent to the side street. Among the reconstructed frame outbuildings are a smokehouse, kitchen, laundry, lumber house, poultry house, well, dovecote, and stable. The pleasure garden is lined with tree box topiaries and ends in an arbor of horn-beams. Two "necessary houses," or privies, are nearby. The orchard and the kitchen garden are on the south side of the property. The house and gardens are open to ticket holders.

■**Weavers** make all sorts of cloth from wool, flax (linen), cotton, hemp, and silk. For most of the time Williamsburg was Virginia's capital, the vast majority of cloth used by its residents was manufactured in England. When the Revolution began, it was necessary to manufacture cloth here. In the late fall of 1776, a plant called the Williamsburg Manu-factory was complete or nearing completion just a few steps from Capitol Landing on Queen's Creek. Today, the weaver has set up shop at the George Wythe House. Besides the manufacture of cloth, you will also find textile coloring done in the eighteenth-century manner with a myriad of fascinating dyes such as insects, spices, nuts, roots, and tree barks. You can see looms, spinning wheels, dyes, yarns, and cloth.

■**Basketmakers** work behind the Wythe House. Baskets were the lightweight, utili-tarian carrying containers of the eighteenth century. Merchants imported some from England, but many farmers and their families made their own, most often from split white oak. Baskets were made in sizes to suit their users, and they were used for a variety of tasks from gathering eggs to hauling potatoes to doing field work.

■*Elkanah Deane Shop*

Elkanah Deane House

MEET . . . GEORGE WYTHE

Although the name of George Wythe (1726–1806) may be less familiar than those of other patriots, he was one of the most influential men of the Revolutionary era. As a member and then clerk of the House of Burgesses, Wythe (rhymes with "Smith") helped lead the patriot movement in Virginia. As one of the colony's delegates to the Continental Congress, he supported independence at Philadelphia. His name appears first among Virginia signers of the Declaration of Independence. Two years later, he helped revise Virginia's laws.

George Wythe's influence as a teacher of law and adviser equaled his distinguished record of public service. He probably did more to shape Thomas Jefferson's ideas than any other man. Jefferson studied law under Wythe and later referred to him as "my faithful and beloved Mentor in youth, and my most affectionate friend through life." Wythe bequeathed his "books and small philosophical apparatus" and his "silver cups and goldheaded cane" to Jefferson.

In 1779, Wythe was appointed to the newly established chair of law at the College of William and Mary, becoming the first individual to hold such a chair at an American university. His students included John Marshall who made an indelible mark on the interpretation of the U.S. Constitution as chief justice of the Supreme Court from 1801 to 1835.

Wythe probably moved into the George Wythe House after he married Elizabeth Taliaferro (pronounced "Tolliver") around 1755. His father-in-law, Colonel Richard Taliaferro, who is believed to have designed the dwelling, bequeathed the couple use of the property for life. Elizabeth Wythe died in 1787, but Wythe continued to live in the house until 1791 when he resigned his professorship and moved to Richmond to serve as a chancery judge.

George Wythe opposed slavery in principle and freed some of his slaves during his lifetime. He taught at least two of his slaves to read.

Wythe died in 1806. He likely was poisoned by George Wythe Sweeney, a ne'er-do-well grandnephew who lived with him. Sweeney probably expected a substantial inheritance, but Wythe lived long enough to disinherit him. Sweeney was never convicted, in part because it was illegal in Virginia for Lydia Broadnax, Wythe's free black housekeeper and an eyewitness to the crime, to testify against a white man.

ICEHOUSE
MOUNT
MAZE
CANAL
FRUIT GARDEN
BALLROOM GARDEN
BOWLING GREEN
11
GRAVEYARD
12
12
TERRACES
KITCHEN GARDEN
10
8
7 6
5 4
3
2
1
FORECOURT
1
9
R
C
13
15
14
ENTRANCE
EXIT

LOOKING NORTH

SECTION

5

The Governor's Palace

Section 5		R	Restrooms
Admission Ticket Required		C	Public Telephones
Places to Shop		D	Cold Drinks
Other Places to Visit		▲	Water Fountains
Exhibition Gardens		X	Buy Tickets Here
Places to Dine		✳	Original Building
Lodging		♿	Accessible to Those with Disabilities
Services or Privately Occupied			

1. Advance buildings
2. Governor's Palace
3. Food and beverage cellars
4. Bagnio (Bathhouse)
5. Laundry
6. Salthouse
7. Smokehouse
8. Kitchen
9. Scullery
10. Privy
11. Toolhouse
12. Privies
13. State coach house
14. Stable
15. Coach house (Wheelwright)

LOOKING NORTH

▪THE GOVERNOR'S PALACE

*A*t the time of its completion in 1722, the residence of Virginia's royal governor was considered one of the finest such buildings in British America. It is difficult to appreciate just how remarkable this building really was unless the rural character of the colony at the close of the seventeenth century is taken into consideration. Despite previous attempts to legislate towns into existence, few real towns or centers of commerce existed in Virginia; instead, the colony was populated by widely scattered agricultural settlements that acquired goods through direct trade with shippers and necessary services as needed from rural tradespeople.

The majority of Virginians, even many who were relatively well-to-do, lived in one-story houses composed of no more than two or three rooms. The enclosing walls of these houses often consisted of posts set directly into the earth and given a crude covering of "riven," or split, boards. Interior plaster and glass windows were found only in houses of the "better sort." By today's standards, living conditions in Virginia at the close of the seventeenth century were modest indeed.

With its broad, straight thoroughfares and massive public buildings, Williamsburg represented a new beginning—a magnet around which the colony would gather itself and thrive. Unlike most towns in Europe, this new metropolis had been laid out around an orderly ensemble of public buildings related to one another in a grand overall scheme.

The Governor's Palace was an important element in this great civic design. Sited at the end of a broad, imposing green, the governor's residence terminated the primary north-south axis of the town. The high visibility and symmetrical formality of this complex did much to reinforce the importance of the governorship in the eyes of Virginians.

Alexander Spotswood assumed the lieutenant governorship with apparent relish in 1710. More than any other of his contemporaries, Spotswood was determined that the new metropolis (and the governor's house in particular) should affirm the dignity and authority of the colony's educational, religious, and governmental institutions.

Soon after he arrived in Williamsburg, Spotswood set about to effect a series of improvements in the plans for the Palace, all of which were intended to amplify its grandeur and enhance his own posture as the Crown's appointed representative. The formal vista along Palace Street toward Francis Street, the elaborate gardens with a canal and falling terraces, the enclosed forecourt with its iron gate and royal heraldic beasts, the magnificent displays of arms in the halls, and the elegant appointments of the upper middle room where the governor received petitioners were features that appear to have been introduced during Spotswood's time.

From the foot of the green at Duke of Gloucester Street to the inner sanctum of Spotswood's receiving rooms, the Palace complex was a carefully orchestrated procession of spaces moving toward and culminating in the presence of the man sworn to uphold the authority of the English monarch in Virginia. The architectural setting of the governor's residence was intended to instill in the colonists respect for executive power and prerogative.

The construction of the Governor's Palace began in 1706, during the administration of Governor Edward Nott. In June of that year, following repeated exhortations from the Crown, the General Assembly voted to build a residence for the governor and appropriated three thousand pounds toward its erection.

Construction proceeded slowly, however, and the house was little more than an enclosed shell when Spotswood arrived in June 1710. Almost immediately the new governor took charge of the project, pushing it forward vigorously. It was almost certainly at his urging that the Assembly enacted additional legislation providing for the enclosure of the forecourt and gardens and considered further recommendations for "rendering the new House Convenient as well as Ornamental." In October 1711, William Byrd of Westover plantation strolled across town to view the new house where he saw a magnificent display of weapons in the entrance hall, "nicely posited," as one observer put it, "by the ingenious contrivance of Colonel Spotswood."

Spotswood had moved into the house by 1716, although the work continued for another six years. In the meantime, the governor turned his attention to the gardens where, in the western part, he laid out a series of terraces that descend to a canal below. Before long, however, members of the Assembly expressed alarm at the money being spent for these refinements. In disgust, Spotswood removed himself entirely from any further involvement with the house and grounds.

The house was finally completed by 1722, but minor repairs and even alterations continued to be made on a regular basis. The Governor's Palace had fallen into such "ruinous condition" by 1751 that Lieutenant Governor Robert Dinwiddie was forced to take up quarters next door at the house owned by Dr. Kenneth McKenzie (now the Robert Carter House) while extensive repairs were undertaken. By 1752, the Palace had been sufficiently rehabilitated to receive the governor and his household. The real construction work had only begun, however. During the ensuing months, a rear wing encompassing the present ballroom and supper room was erected under the supervision of Richard Taliaferro, who was also responsible for the construction of the George Wythe House.

The creation of two large rooms for public entertainments coincided with the construction of similar spaces elsewhere in Williamsburg. The "great room" at Wetherburn's Tavern, where Governor Dinwiddie was first entertained after taking office, is believed to have been completed in 1751, as was the Apollo Room at the Raleigh Tavern. Such rooms were being added to private residences as well. The elaborate downstairs room at the Peyton Randolph House appears to date from the same era.

The entrance hall in the Governor's Palace.

This new desire for large rooms suited to public entertainments echoed a similar trend in England. In 1756, English architect Isaac Ware noted that the addition of a "great room" to private residences had become commonplace, complaining that such an addition "always hangs from one end, or sticks to one side, of the house, and shews to the most careless eye, that, though fastened to the walls it does not belong to the building."

After the completion of the ballroom wing, few changes of any importance occurred in or around the Palace until the arrival of Norborne Berkeley, Baron de Botetourt, in 1768. Shortly after assuming his post, the governor launched a thorough program of redecoration.

The last royal governor, John Murray, fourth Earl of Dunmore, was joined by his wife and six of their children in Williamsburg

Becoming Americans
Our Struggle to Be Both Free and Equal

THE FIRST CONSUMER REVOLUTION

Some programs in the Historic Area examine the changes that simultaneously revolutionized trade and technology and ultimately transformed peoples' standards and styles of living at all levels of society.

During the Middle Ages everyday domestic life among all classes except the nobility involved little in the way of clothing, furniture, and other household equipment. A person's reputation was measured by the land, labor, and livestock everyone knew he owned. By 1700, however, growing numbers of ordinary people in northern Europe and America began demanding and acquiring newly available consumer goods, using services, and engaging in social, recreational, and educational activities that went far beyond meeting or improving their basic physical needs.

Seeking respectability within an increasingly mobile society, successful image makers in Virginia dressed in the latest London fashions and built houses suitable for entertaining. They furnished those houses with new, specialized forms of furniture. They took tea from fashionable tea wares. Adults and children learned the rules of behavior that reaffirmed their social positions and differentiated them from their "inferiors." By midcentury local tradesmen and merchants—supported by advances in British business practices and industrial technology—offered an ever-increasing variety of consumer goods and services.

Widespread possession of store-bought culture, combined with etiquette book manners, contributed to a novel idea: equality, the belief in everyone's equal worth and right to pursue a better life. Yet some rejected the new materialism and the notion of equality. Others—especially the poor, slaves, and servants—were disadvantaged by it. Resulting clashes between the haves and have-nots, slave and free, men and women, country and city, and different religious groups were resolved in many ways. The widely shared experience of consumption eventually helped Americans of varying backgrounds express with a single voice their opposition to Parliament and its unjust laws.

on February 26, 1774. Another child had died in 1773, and one infant, considered too fragile to travel, had been left in England. Their ninth child, named Virginia in honor of the colony, was born in the Palace in December 1774. Botetourt had been a bachelor. Dunmore's family life changed the use of several rooms in the Palace and also necessitated additional upgrades beyond those Botetourt carried out.

The family was received with a great deal of ceremony and delight by the residents of Williamsburg, with fireworks, illuminations, balls, and poems composed for the occasion. The two older boys were enrolled at the College of William and Mary grammar school, boarding at the college. The oldest son, George, Lord Fincastle, received special instruction there until, with the coming of the American Revolution, Dunmore and his family fled Williamsburg.

The Palace then served as a residence for the first two governors of the new Commonwealth of Virginia, Patrick Henry and Thomas Jefferson. It was probably during his residence in Williamsburg that Jefferson prepared a series of drawings to guide in remodeling the Palace. His proposed changes were never carried out, however, because the seat of government—and the governor's residence—moved to Richmond in 1780.

American forces used the vacant Palace as a hospital following the siege of Yorktown. The orchard terrace overlooking the canal became a burial ground for 156 American soldiers. On the night of December 22, 1781, fire broke out in the Palace, and in three hours it had burned to the ground. Shortly afterward, all that remained of the central structure's charred hulk was pulled down, and the bricks were sold. Within a few short months, the once-great Palace of Virginia's royal governors had become only a memory, its flanking advance buildings and outlying dependencies tangible reminders of its vanished magnificence.

In the eighteenth century, a liveried footman showed callers at the Palace into the entrance hall, where large quantities of muskets, swords, and pistols were impressively displayed on the walls. First installed by Governor Spotswood in 1715, this arms arrangement served not only as a symbol of royal authority but also as a supplementary arsenal to the Powder Magazine.

Like those royal guard chambers, the hall at the Palace functioned as a screening area where visitors wishing to see the governor were "sorted out." The butler supervised this process, having his office in the pantry to the left of the front door. From this vantage point, he also managed the household staff, which consisted of more than two dozen servants and slaves. Hanging on the door is a ring of keys, a reminder that the butler along with the housekeeper also controlled access to the governor's valuable collection of silver and to his stocks of wine and food in the cellar. Beside the library table where household accounts were kept is a daybed in which the butler could have rested while protecting the contents of this important room.

The parlor on the right served Dunmore as a business area, with a small space reserved for his private secretary or chief of staff, Edward Foy. The majority of official business was carried out in one of the advance buildings. James Minzies, clerk of the governor's office during Dunmore's tenure, had his office in the East Advance Building and lived above it.

The ornamental display of firearms and swords extended up the stairs to the second story of the Palace. Beyond these stairs, a formal receiving room was part of the grand progression of spaces required for eighteenth-century aristocratic protocol. The earl and the countess probably had separate bedchambers. While "levees," formal ceremonies to welcome and entertain guests, had traditionally been held in the upper middle room, this receiving room also might have been used by the family when the countess visited with her children during the day. Those who enjoyed a close friendship with the governor or countess might be invited into their bedchambers, each of which also would have contained a dressing closet.

The countess also required space for household management, correspondence, and private time. Although she had a full retinue of servants, including her chaplain, the Reverend Mr. Gwatkin, and her waiting maid, Elizabeth Ruth, the responsibilities as chatelaine of the palace and first lady of the colony were complicated by pregnancy, childbirth, and the uncertainties of this turbulent period on the eve of the Revolution. The roles and contributions of women, from countess to housekeeper, cook, and chambermaid, though rigidly defined, have often been minimized.

The six chambers on the third story would have been occupied by children; the nurse, Mary Thompson; and perhaps the governess, Francotte Galli. An additional story over the ballroom might also have contained chambers for family and other servants. Dunmore's loyalist claim when he left Virginia accounted for fifty-seven slaves and twelve indentured servants. Despite the formality of life in the Palace compound, the hustle and bustle of so many children, servants, and visitors would have enlivened every space.

The dining room was perceived as a masculine domain, from which ladies typically withdrew after meals, leaving the men to their bottles and tobacco. In some cases, the decor of dining rooms in colonial Virginia reflected this masculine character. At Mount Airy, Colonel John Tayloe covered the dining room walls with portraits of English racehorses. While Botetourt often granted public audiences in his dining room, a space he dedicated as much to business and politics as to meals, Lord Dunmore and his wife and children would have gathered here for large family meals as well as to entertain with considerable pomp.

A glass pyramid dressed for the dessert course graces the table in the Palace dining room.

Food brought over from the kitchen on covered pewter platters was transferred to china and silver serving pieces and garnished in the little middle room before being taken into the dining room across the passage.

Many visitors at the Palace enjoyed the governor's entertainments. From the entrance hall, visitors passed through the set of double doors leading into the ballroom, where dances, or "assemblies" (as those occasions were sometimes called), took place.

Among the most fashionable and up-to-date rooms in the building, the ballroom and supper room became a stage on which the governor and his guests acted out the latest forms of etiquette and displayed themselves as being in touch with the world's most fashionable and civilized conversation and manners. Early in the eighteenth century, such an event would have involved a relatively small group of people, all engaged in a single activity in one room. Later in the century, however, assemblies included many more people and featured a variety of activities going on in separate rooms. While people danced in one room and played cards in another, refreshments or a light supper might be served in yet another.

At the far end of the supper room, a last pair of doors leads visitors into a formal garden resembling those found on many English estates during the early eighteenth century. Quite often those formal gardens served to frame pleasing views of distant pastoral scenery. This distant landscape, called a "park," was in many cases planted with clumps of trees arranged informally for a picturesque effect. Grazing cattle or a herd of deer usually completed the scene. By providing pleasant prospects, or vistas, to be enjoyed from near the house, the park functioned as an important adjunct to the formal garden.

Just such a park, which encompassed sixty-three acres, complemented the governor's gardens. Like many of its English counterparts, this park was visible from a mount in the formal garden or as visitors looked northward through the delicate tracery of the great wrought-iron gate.

The formal garden with its manicured plantings was equally important as a source of pleasurable recreation. Here gentlemen might stroll along fragrant walks, trading pleasant flatteries with the ladies or perhaps continuing a conversation begun over dinner. Above all, however, these impressive gardens helped to present the governor as a refined and important man. In this respect, they functioned as an extension of the house and mirrored its formal character.

Farther from the house, in the westernmost part of the garden, Spotswood's terraces, planted in a less formal manner than the rest of the garden, fall gently to the fish pond below. Spotswood capitalized on the topographic variety of the site, an approach to gardening that gained favor in England as designers began to move away from the rigid formality of an earlier age. Credit for the gardens also belonged to a slave known

as James. He was such a skilled gardener that several governors used him.

The service yards are located to the east and west of the advance buildings that flank the Palace. The elegance of the governor's residence did not just happen; it was the product of hard work by many servants—butlers, footmen, maids, cooks, laundresses, gardeners, grooms, and laborers. The kitchen, scullery, laundry, and other support buildings involved in the task of maintaining the household are in the west yard. Of special interest is the hexagonal "bagnio," or bathhouse, a luxury rarely found elsewhere in Virginia.

The kitchen was among the finest in Virginia. Here, today's Historic Foodways staff demonstrates the high style of cooking. You can also learn about brewing, butchering, and chocolate making at the ■Palace Kitchen.

The stables and carriage house in the east yard served the transportation needs of the household. Lord Botetourt's state coach, a heavily gilded ceremonial vehicle in which the governor rode to the Capitol to open sessions of the General Assembly, was kept in the coach house. The elegance of His Excellency's coach prompted one visitor to comment on the tendency of Virginians "to adopt ideas of royalty and magnificence."

Today, ■wheelwrights demonstrate their trade in the stable area. In the eighteenth century, wheeled vehicles of every kind—wheelbarrows, riding chairs, carriages, and carts—were needed to move people or possessions from place to place. Wheeled vehicles of every description could be seen in the streets of Virginia's colonial capital.

The wheelwright must craft precise woodworking joints to bring the hub, spokes, and rim sections together into a perfectly round wheel. These parts are compressed tightly by an iron tire around the wheel's circumference to give it strength and durability. In the shop today, the wheelwrights produce wheels for the vehicles used in the Historic Area.

The map shows the area including Richmond Road, Jamestown Road, College of William and Mary with the Wren Building, President's House, Brafferton, Duke of Gloucester Street, Merchants Square, Kimball Theatre, Everything Williamsburg, Williamsburg at Home, Williamsburg Craft House, Williamsburg Celebrations, Merchants Ticket office, Boundary Street, Henry Street, and Francis Street.

FROM PALACE GREEN TO THE COLLEGE OF WILLIAM AND MARY

An asterisk indicates that a building is an original eighteenth- or nineteenth-century structure. A blue box indicates that you need an admission ticket to see an attraction.

For most of the seventeenth century, what is now Williamsburg was little more than a winding horse path faced by a tavern, a few stores, and several houses. Two important institutions fostered the growth of this part of the street. The first, Bruton Parish, formed in 1674. The second, the colony's new college named to honor King William and Queen Mary of England, was chartered in 1693. These two institutions, less than a half-mile apart, drew workers, artisans, and businessmen to Middle Plantation, the sparsely settled outpost that had been established in 1633 on the ridge between the James and York Rivers.

The appeal of locating the center of government near the colony's center of learning was partly responsible for the General Assembly's

STREET

*Bowden-Armistead House

*Bruton Parish Church

James Geddy Foundry

D

*Roscow Cole House

John Blair ***House and Kitchen**

PALACE STREET

PALACE GREEN

PALACE STREET

James Geddy House   **Mary Dickinson Store**

GLOUCESTER STREET

X **John Greenhow Store**

quare ice

Durfey Shop

Catherine Blaikley House

Bryan House

NASSAU STREET

*Taliaferro-Cole House

*Taliaferro-Cole Shop (Harnessmaker-Saddler)

Hartwell Perry's Tavern

Colonial Garden and Nursery

Custis Tenement

John Greenhow Lumber House

John Greenhow House

Shoemaker's Shop

Greenhow Tenement

*Greenhow Brick Office

Taliaferro-Cole Stable (African American Religion Exhibit)

STREET

0   100   200   300   400 FEET

SECTION

6

From Palace Green to the College

☐ Section 6	**R** Restrooms
☐ Admission Ticket Required	**C** Public Telephones
☐ Places to Shop	**D** Cold Drinks
■ Other Places to Visit	▲ Water Fountains
▒ Exhibition Gardens	**X** Buy Tickets Here
■ Places to Dine	***** Original Building
☐ Lodging	♿ Accessible to Those with Disabilities
▒ Services or Privately Occupied	

choice in 1699 of Middle Plantation as the site of the new capital. In practical terms, the great hall at the college provided a convenient meeting place for the legislature until a proper Capitol building could be erected. A major transformation of the town, renamed Williamsburg in honor of the English monarch, began. The grounds of the Capitol were located about a mile east of the college, with Duke of Gloucester Street linking the two buildings. The old path was widened and straightened, and any buildings standing in the new roadway were removed.

This "uptown" section of Williamsburg took on a more residential appearance than the busier "downtown" blocks of Duke of Gloucester Street near the Capitol. After the government moved to Richmond in 1780, commercial activity at the eastern end of the street declined. The college and the Public Hospital became Williamsburg's major local institutions, and the focus of town life shifted to this part of the city.

James Geddy
*House and *Foundry*

Mary Dickinson
Store

FROM PALACE STREET TO NASSAU STREET

From about 1737 to 1777, gunsmith James Geddy Sr. and his sons lived at or operated shops on the site of the ■James Geddy House and ■Foundry. A good deal more than gunsmithing went on here, however. An inventory taken after Geddy's death lists shop equipment, including brasswork for guns, a turner's lathe, bullet molds, and gunsmith's, cutler's, and founder's tools. In 1751, Geddy's sons David and William advertised that they were carrying on these trades at the shop near Bruton Parish Church.

In 1760, the widowed Anne Geddy sold the property to her son James Jr. who set up shop as a silversmith, goldsmith, and watch repairer. He also sold and repaired jewelry and objects of silver. It was difficult to attract customers to a location so far away from the busy Capitol. In a 1771 advertisement, a concerned Geddy hoped that the reasonableness of his prices would "remove the Objection of his Shop's being too high up Town . . . and the Walk may be thought rather an Amusement than a Fatigue."

William Waddill, a journeyman silversmith and engraver, worked in Geddy's shop. In 1770, Waddill made eight silver handles, a large engraved nameplate, and sixteen escutcheons for royal governor Lord Botetourt's coffin. James Geddy Jr. married Elizabeth Waddill, probably William's sister. A leader in the community, James Geddy was one of three artisans named to the Williamsburg common council.

The two-story L-shaped Geddy House dates from the 1760s. Its low-pitched roof without dormers and the front porch with balcony and doorway above are unusual features. Today, interpretations in the house focus on the domestic and commercial activities of the family of James Geddy Jr.

The Geddys operated a foundry behind the house. In the eighteenth century, the yard around several busy forges would have been littered with piles of coal, mounds of slag, and assorted iron and brass waste. A foundry once again operates on the property as artisans cast objects in bronze, brass, pewter, and silver.

Mary Dickinson advertised millinery, jewelry, and other goods for sale "next Door to MR. JAMES GEDDY'S Shop, near the Church" in an October 1771 issue of the *Virginia Gazette*. Today, an elegant assortment of items is again available in the **Mary Dickinson Store.**

The frame **Greenhow Tenement,** across and down the street from the Geddy House, was once the property of John Greenhow, whose son sold it to printer and newspaper publisher Joseph Repiton in 1810.

In 1773, George Wilson & Company advertised the arrival of a "choice Cargo of the best sorts of English leather for all Manner of Mens Shoes and Pumps" at the ■**Shoemaker's Shop.** Wilson must have had more business than he could handle, since he encouraged two or three journeymen shoemakers to apply to him "next Door to Mr. Greenhow's Store in Williamsburg." By the end of the next year,

however, the household furniture and working materials of George Wilson, deceased, were offered for sale.

An eighteenth-century shoemaker could average one pair of shoes per day. He made them with round or pointed toes as fashion might decree, although he generally used a straight last—that is, without distinction between right and left. Today, tradespeople once again make shoes here using the tools and techniques of the eighteenth century.

One contemporary account described the home of John Greenhow, a merchant in Williamsburg from about 1755 to his death in 1787, as "a large and commodious Dwelling House." The adjoining **John Greenhow Store** is the most completely reconstructed eighteenth-century commercial space in Williamsburg. From the merchant's counting room in back to the freshly painted sign above the front door, the store is an authentic re-creation of its eighteenth-century counterpart. Advertisements in the *Virginia Gazette* from 1766 to 1780 enabled researchers to identify the wide variety of goods that John Greenhow and his sons sold in their general store. Wrought iron, fabrics, cooper's items, tinware, "and almost every other useful article that can be thought of" are featured here again today.

Viewed from the street, the building appears to be in three segments. From left to

Greenhow Tenement ■ *Shoemaker's Shop*

MEET . . . CATHERINE RATHELL

Catherine Rathell came to Virginia from London in 1765 or 1766 "with a view of setting up a Milliners Shop at Williamsburg." Although she initially settled in Fredericksburg, Mrs. Rathell traveled to the capital during legislative and court sessions to sell goods here. By 1768, she had opened a shop in Williamsburg and was also taking in lodgers. An active businesswoman, Mrs. Rathell went wherever customers could be found. She opened a shop in Annapolis in 1769 and intended to open one in Petersburg in 1772, but she always came back to Williamsburg.

Mrs. Rathell's stock in trade included a variety of fashionable goods imported from London. She sold items such as fabric, lace, fans, ribbons, jewelry, buttons, gloves, shoes, spoons, hats, caps, canes, and riding whips. She was very particular about the quality of her goods, insisting that they be "the very best & most fashionable goods in Williamsburg." When she could, Mrs. Rathell traveled to London to choose merchandise herself. At other times, she ordered through a London merchant house.

In protest against British policies toward the colonies, the Continental Congress passed a resolution in October 1774 forbidding the importation of British goods. Local committees were elected to enforce the boycott. This resolution was disastrous for those whose livelihoods depended on being able to import British products. In April 1775, milliner and merchant Catherine Rathell announced her intention to return to England "till Liberty of Importation is allowed." She boarded the ship *Peggy* and set sail. The ship sank within sight of the port of Liverpool. All the passengers, including Mrs. Rathell, perished.

---

right, there are a sloped-roof counting room and office for the proprietor, the entrance to the store, and the doorway to the **John Greenhow House.** The separate building to the right, whose gable end faces the street, is the **John Greenhow Lumber House.** It functioned as a stockroom for furniture, barrels, and odds and ends too bulky to keep in the store itself. In eighteenth-century parlance, "lumber" meant "items in storage."

The generous size, layout, and exterior finish of the combination store and home and the lumber house are indicated on several early-nineteenth-century fire insurance policies taken out by Greenhow's son Robert. The insurance plats also show that

John Greenhow Store and *House*   *John Greenhow Lumber House*

Paths paved with shells crisscross the Custis Tenement garden in an intricate geometric pattern.

behind the Greenhow property the slope of the ravine—with its meadows, gardens, corn house, and other outbuildings—was put to an agricultural use typical of lots at this end of Duke of Gloucester Street.

The **Custis Tenement** stands on a lot that John Custis acquired in 1714. Custis also purchased two lots to the immediate west, built structures on them, and rented the properties as tenements. Cabinetmaker Peter Scott's residence, for example, was located in the open lot west of the formal garden.

In 1746, Custis leased a house on this lot to carpenter John Wheatley for three years, during which time Wheatley was to maintain the dwelling in good repair and "continually to keep the Chimneys clean swept for fear of fire." He continued to rent the property through 1757, according to accounts presented in court by Martha Custis, the widow of Daniel Parke Custis, who had inherited the property from his father. The widow Custis later married George Washington.

Just as English and European towns and villages had for centuries grown up around parish churches, so too did Middle Plantation. The tombs, gravestones, and site of a modest brick church completed in 1683 are reminders of the small seventeenth-century hamlet that was transformed into Williamsburg by Governor Nicholson's plan for a new city designed to be a fit seat for the colonial capital of Virginia.

In the late seventeenth century, before the college was built, **Bruton Parish Church** was the most important public building at Middle Plantation. Named for a town in Somerset, England, Bruton Parish was established when several smaller parishes were joined together in 1674. Three years later, the vestry ordered that a church be built in Middle Plantation. A

Custis Tenement

small buttressed brick church was completed in 1683. Francis Louis Michel, a Swiss traveler who visited Williamsburg in 1702, left a sketch of the first Bruton Parish Church that shows it had curvilinear end gables done in the Flemish manner. Its foundations are marked by granite posts northwest of the present church.

The small church was badly in need of repair by the early 1700s. Furthermore, it could not accommodate the many people who came to town during "Publick Times" when the courts were convened. The vestrymen therefore petitioned the General Assembly "for their Generous contribution" toward building a new church. Lieutenant Governor Alexander Spotswood, an architectural enthusiast, provided a "platt or draught of the Church," and the Assembly, which wanted a building more appropriate for the seat of government, appropriated two hundred pounds toward the cost. Begun in 1712, the cruciform Bruton Parish Church has been in continuous use since 1715.

James Morris, carpenter, supervised the construction of the church. Other Williamsburg artisans also worked on the structure; for example, Lewis Delony built the pews and John Tyler oversaw the building and finishing of the north and south wings.

The chancel was extended twenty-two feet to the east in 1752 and an English organ was installed in 1755. The stone baptismal font reportedly was brought from an earlier church at Jamestown about this time. In 1769, local contractor Benjamin Powell was awarded the contract to build a tower and steeple. The much darker shade of the bricks used in the tower contrasts with the soft salmon color of the brickwork of the main building. The bell, given to the parish by merchant James Tarpley in 1761, is still in use today.

From 1903 to 1907, under the direction of then-rector Dr. W. A. R. Goodwin, nineteenth-century changes were stripped from the church to return the interior to the way it had looked in the 1700s. A more complete restoration occurred in 1940. The building's walls and windows are original, as is the west gallery where students from the college sat. The initials they carved in the handrail are still discernible.

The churchyard was surrounded by a brick wall in 1754. Many graves, including that of Governor Edward Nott, are located in the churchyard. Governor Francis Fauquier is buried inside the church. In the eighteenth

Bruton Parish Church

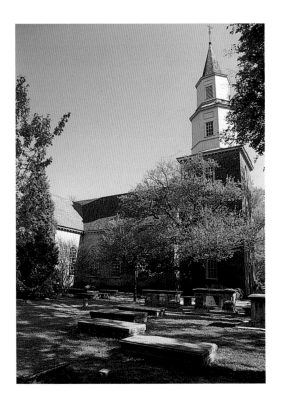

Divine services were held each Sunday morning. They included readings from the Book of Common Prayer, a sermon, and, four times a year, the taking of holy communion. Services were also held on Christmas Day, Good Friday, and various saint's days. It is thought that some favored house slaves sat with their owners in the pews.

Blacks in the parish also worshipped at Bruton Parish Church. Tradition says that they sat apart in the north gallery, although it is possible they were relegated to floor space on the periphery or to back benches. By the end of the Revolution, more than one thousand slaves, many of them infants, had been baptized in Bruton Parish.

Inspired by two black preachers, first Moses and then Gowan Pamphlet, a number of Williamsburg-area blacks, most of them slaves, formed a church of their own during the Revolution. With a membership of five hundred, "the Baptist Church of black people at Williamsburg" was received into the Dover Baptist Association, a white-run regional organization, in 1793. A plaque marks the site of the original church on Nassau Street opposite the Taliaferro-Cole Stable, which houses the African American Religion Exhibit.

The **Bowden-Armistead House,** completed in 1858 of Baltimore stock brick, is a good example of Greek Revival architecture. The iron fence that surrounds it was brought from Richmond.

Lemuel J. Bowden, a lawyer and president of the board of overseers of Eastern State Hospital, purchased the land on which the house stands from Bruton Parish. Many town residents considered Bowden, one of Williamsburg's few Northern sympathizers during the Civil War, to be a traitor and gave him the unflattering nickname "Virginia Yankee." In 1874, the house was purchased from the Bowden estate by lawyer Robert T. Armistead. It is still owned by the Armistead family today.

century, however, it was more often the custom for people to be buried at home in private cemeteries. The Reverend Hugh Jones complained about this practice in 1724 because it meant he had to travel long distances to officiate at burials. Typical private plots can be seen today behind the Custis Tenement and the Taliaferro-Cole House across the street. Some of the table tombs in the churchyard were imported from England.

The Church of England was the official church in colonial Virginia. Made up of twelve men, the vestry regulated church affairs and determined the annual taxes necessary to pay the minister's salary set by law, provide relief for the poor of the parish, and repair the church. Free Virginians were required by law to attend divine services at least once each month and could be fined for failure to do so. All officeholders were obliged to conform to the established church, and all taxpayers—Anglicans and dissenters alike—were required by law to support it.

Bowden-Armistead House

At the **Colonial Garden and Nursery**, across from Bruton Parish Church, interpreters demonstrate eighteenth-century gardening techniques. Plant varieties found in Williamsburg during the colonial era and eighteenth-century-style tools and horticultural supplies are also for sale here.

Hartwell Perry's Tavern was named for Hartwell Perry who owned and operated an "ordinary," as colonial taverns were sometimes called, on this site from the mid-1780s until he died about 1800. The sign hanging out front is a rebus. It depicts a deer, a well, and several pears. "Hart" is another name for a deer, and an alcoholic beverage made from pears is called "perry"—so the sign stands for Hartwell Perry.

Despite a late-nineteenth-century facade and earlier additions to the rear, the original ■**Taliaferro-Cole Shop** had remained essentially intact when the building was acquired for restoration.

Coachmaker Charles Taliaferro practiced his trade in Williamsburg for more than thirty years. He also operated a brewery and a warehouse, hired out boats, and sold foodstuffs and other supplies to outfit ships at nearby College Landing. He purchased this property in the early 1770s. The western section of the **Taliaferro-Cole House** dates from Taliaferro's period of ownership, but the restored house reflects the early 1800s, when Jesse Cole acquired the house and shop. Cole used the shop as a post office and general store. He also allowed Gowan Pamphlet's black Baptist congregation to meet on his property. Today, the shop houses the trades of the **harnessmaker** and the **saddler** while the nearby stable is home to the ■**African American Religion Exhibit**. The stable is across the street from the site of the nineteenth-century church building.

Hartwell Perry's Tavern   ■*Taliaferro-Cole Shop* (Harnessmaker-Saddler)   *Taliaferro-Cole House*

*John Blair House

John Blair Kitchen

FROM NASSAU STREET TO HENRY STREET

The Frenchman's map (see page 16) shows that by the late 1700s a house existed where the **Bryan House** now stands. By the end of the century it was owned by William Bryan, and it survived until early in the twentieth century, at different times serving as a grocery store, school, and residence. In reconstructing the gable-roofed house, architects were guided by photographs and recollections of Williamsburg residents as well as archaeological records.

William Blaikley and his wife, Catherine, lived in the **Catherine Blaikley House** next door. When he died in 1736, William bequeathed "unto my loving wife Catherine Blaikley, all my whole estate of lands, houses, negroes, goods, and chattels." Catherine, who never remarried, remained at this address until her death in 1771 at the age of seventy-three. A remarkable woman, she was renowned as

an "eminent Midwife . . . who, in the course of her Practice, brought upwards of three thousand Children into the world."

In April 1773, tailor Severinus Durfey announced his move to the house formerly occupied by Mrs. Blaikley. He used the **Durfey Shop** to the west for his tailoring activities and for other commercial purposes. The golden fleece of the signboard is the traditional symbol of a tailor's shop.

The **John Blair House** and **Kitchen** on the north side of Duke of Gloucester Street was the home of a prominent family of Virginians. The Reverend James Blair (1655–1743), founder and first president of the College of William and Mary, came to Virginia in 1685. His brother Dr. Archibald Blair arrived in 1690. Archibald's son, John Blair Sr., received a legacy of ten thousand pounds from his uncle James, who also left his library and five hundred pounds to the college.

John Blair Sr. (1689–1771), a burgess and auditor general of the colony from 1728 to

Bryan House

Catherine Blaikley House   Durfey Shop

Becoming Americans
Our Struggle to Be Both Free and Equal

LAND

While struggling with the British government's expanding imperial policies, eighteenth-century Virginians pursued land ownership even as Native Americans sought to retain control of their ancestral homes. Competition to possess the land shaped a number of fundamental American values.

Throughout the colonial period, the promise of land ownership lured a steady stream of European immigrants to the colony. By the 1770s, Virginians had pushed westward, reaching the Ohio River Valley and Kentucky.

In their eagerness to claim the land, Virginians repeatedly came into contact—and conflict—with its native inhabitants. For native peoples, the land and its traditional uses were at the center of their culture. For colonists, land ownership was vital to their economic independence and social advancement.

As the capital of a vast territory, Williamsburg was the center of shifting networks of political, economic, diplomatic, and military relationships that linked colonial Virginia, Native American groups, other colonies, and France and Great Britain as each vied for control of the Ohio country and Kentucky.

In taking possession of the land for themselves, colonial Virginians altered the environment and initiated an exploitative ideology of land usage. The emergence of a large freeholding population fostered Americans' belief in individualism and the ideal of private land ownership. Even so, this privilege has yet to be extended to all Americans.

1771, was appointed to the Council in 1745. Later, as president of the Council, he twice served as acting governor of the colony. His son John Blair Jr. (1732–1800) graduated from the College of William and Mary and studied law at the Middle Temple in London. He was elected to the House of Burgesses and later became clerk of the Council. He sat on the committee that drew up Virginia's Declaration of Rights and first state constitution. He served the new commonwealth as councillor, judge, and chief justice. In 1787, he represented Virginia at the Constitutional Convention where he firmly advocated federal union, and, in 1789, President George Washington appointed him to the U.S. Supreme Court.

The original, easterly part of the John Blair House was built early in the eighteenth century. It is one of the oldest houses in Williamsburg. Town tradition has it that the stone steps at both doors came from the Palace Street theater. The steps were added when the house was lengthened twenty-eight feet to the west sometime during the second quarter of the eighteenth century.

The kitchen, with its huge chimney, has been reconstructed. Between the kitchen and the street is a small formal garden filled with an ever-changing assortment of herbs.

FROM MERCHANTS SQUARE TO THE COLLEGE OF WILLIAM AND MARY

Merchants Square Ticket Office, at the corner of South Henry and Duke of Gloucester Streets, is open daily for information and admission tickets.

The 1782 Frenchman's Map shows quite a few buildings on the last block of Duke of Gloucester Street, the area that is now called **Merchants Square,** but little is known about the people who resided there or the structures in which they lived. Usually a tavern and other businesses catered to the needs of the faculty and students at the College of William and Mary.

Today, Merchants Square is again a busy commercial and shopping district. The stores are modeled after eighteenth- and early-nineteenth-century structures from Maryland and Delaware. More than sixty years old, Merchants Square is one of the first planned shopping centers in America.

Constructed as part of the development of Merchants Square, the Williamsburg Theatre opened in 1933. A generous donation from benefactors Bill and Gretchen Kimball enabled the renovation and expansion of the theater so that it now permits a wide variety of programs and performances. The **Kimball Theatre,** open several days each week, offers performing arts events, educational presentations, and films. Creative programming alliances with the College of William and Mary, community organizations, and Colonial Williamsburg link our rich past with the present. The box office, a Colonial Williamsburg ticket sales location, opens one hour before each event.

The orderly and almost symmetrical area of the **College of William and Mary** yard at the western end of Duke of Gloucester Street forms an architectural unit in itself. The central structure is the **Wren Building,** with its massive chimneys and lofty cupola. Flanking it to the north and south are the **President's House** and the **Brafferton,** buildings apparently identical to one another in dimension and detail, although the Brafferton is actually somewhat smaller. The narrow, many-paned windows and steeply pitched roofs of these two buildings give a strong vertical accent to the architectural composition.

The College of William and Mary is the second oldest institution of higher education in the United States. It received a charter from King William and Queen Mary in 1693 after

Wren Building

the General Assembly sent the Reverend James Blair to England to persuade the royal couple to found an Anglican college in the colony so that "the Church of Virginia may be furnish'd with a Seminary of Ministers of the Gospel." The college was also established in order "that the Youth may be piously educated in good Letters and Manners, and the Christian Faith may be propagated amongst the Western Indians."

In the eighteenth century, a higher education was not easily acquired in the colonies, so the few who attained it enjoyed considerable prestige. Plantation owners commonly entrusted their young sons to tutors who lived with the family. Occasionally, a few studied with a clergyman who augmented his income by running a small school. Several Virginia

gentry boys went to English boarding schools. Young men then obtained a higher education by attending the College of William and Mary or going overseas to study at the universities of Oxford, Cambridge, or Edinburgh. Some read law at the Inns of Court in London.

Although the average enrollment during the eighteenth century was less than one hundred, the College of William and Mary greatly influenced the intellectual life of Virginia. The college produced an extraordinary number of distinguished alumni, including Thomas Jefferson, John Marshall, and James Monroe.

Students at the college received a classical education. The grammar school admitted boys of about age twelve. They prepared for college-level work by mastering Latin and Greek as well as mathematics, geography, and

MEET . . . JOHN NETTLES

In the early 1770s, John Nettles, a young college student, was summoned before the faculty of the College of William and Mary for getting drunk at a Williamsburg tavern. He had committed a common offense, yet the master of the Indian school was clearly upset with Nettles. This promising young man had met the faculty's expectations. That he would risk all he had achieved by this misstep was alarming because Nettles was no ordinary student. He was a Catawba Indian, and he was expected to bring Christianity and civilization to his people.

Since the early eighteenth century, the college had enrolled Indian youngsters at the Brafferton, where they were taught reading, writing, and arithmetic. The young boys were also instructed in Christianity. And, most important, they were to experience firsthand the superiority of English culture. The faculty hoped that when the students returned home, they would continue to live like Englishmen and, by their example, lead their families to abandon their Indian ways.

The faculty's hopes were almost always disappointed. Once home, the young men reverted to their traditional ways. And so did John Nettles. In 1786, he was described as "a perfect Indian."

Although Nettles failed to keep to his instructors' expectations, he did fulfill the goals of the Catawbas. Within the year, the literate John Nettles was carrying messages to the colonial authorities, and he would act as an interpreter between his people and their white neighbors for the next forty years. By playing the middleman, the college-educated Nettles helped the Catawbas maintain their cultural autonomy in what for them was a hostile world.

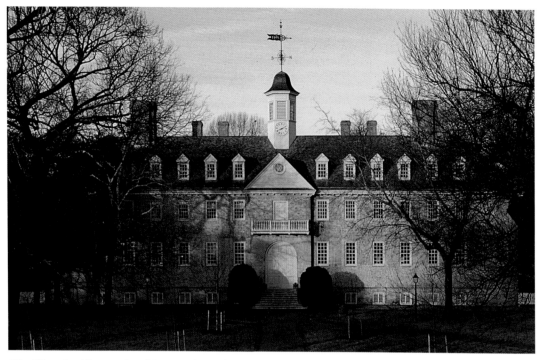

The Wren Building is the oldest academic building in use in America.

penmanship. Latin was the language of both written and spoken classwork.

In addition to logic, rhetoric, and ethics, older students studied natural philosophy—mathematics, physics, and metaphysics. After four years of study in the school of philosophy, young men who submitted a written thesis and made a successful oral defense of it were awarded a bachelor of arts degree. Most students at the college in the eighteenth century left without taking a degree, however.

The faculty included distinguished men such as the Reverend Hugh Jones, mathematician, and Dr. William Small, professor of natural philosophy (science). "I know of no place in the world," wrote Jefferson in 1788, "while the present professors remain, where I would so soon place a son."

It was largely through the influence of alumnus Jefferson that the curriculum was broadened in 1779. To the old professorships of moral philosophy, natural philosophy, and

mathematics were added new chairs of law and police, chemistry and medicine, ethics and belles lettres, and modern languages. The chair of divinity and the grammar school were discontinued. Although the school had been founded as an Anglican college, the Reverend James Madison (cousin of the U. S. president), its president at the time, explained, "It is now thought that Establishments in favor of any particular Sect are incompatible with the Freedom of a Republic."

The Wren Building bears the name of distinguished English architect Sir Christopher Wren, who is credited, perhaps erroneously, with having influenced its original design. Construction began in 1695. The building's front and north wing, which contains a great hall, were completed by 1700. The chapel wing was added in 1732. Although fires in 1705, 1859, and 1862 did serious damage, the massive exterior walls of the Wren Building are largely original. They have withstood

President's House

not only flames but also the architectural modifications and structural alterations that were part of each rebuilding. The Wren Building now has the outward appearance that it showed from early in the eighteenth century until the fire of 1859. It was the first major Williamsburg structure to be restored by John D. Rockefeller Jr.

The courtyard was originally intended to be enclosed within a quadrangular building, the two wings being joined across the far ends by a structure similar to the front side. Jefferson, an accomplished amateur architect, drew plans for an enlarged quadrangle, and foundations had been laid when the outbreak of the Revolution put an end to the project. Some of those foundations still exist.

The president, the professors, and the master of the grammar school ate at the head table in the great hall, the dining room for the college. At the other tables, in descending order of status, sat the students, lesser faculty, "servitors and college officers," and, finally, the Indian master and his pupils. From the kitchen, directly below, the housekeeper saw to it that "plenty of Victuals" were "served up in the cleanest and neatest Manner possible" three times each day.

The House of Burgesses met in the great hall during the years 1700 to 1704 while the Capitol was under construction. The government of Governor Nicholson crowded all of its activities and offices into the building, "to the great disturbance of the College business," President Blair complained. The burgesses met there again from 1747 to 1754 while the Capitol was rebuilt after being gutted by fire.

Added in 1732, the chapel is evidence that the established Church of England played a central role in education as well as government in colonial Virginia. In the crypt below the chapel are buried Sir John Randolph; his sons, Peyton and John; royal governor Lord Botetourt; Bishop James Madison; and several other distinguished Virginians.

Students began the day at six or seven o'clock with morning prayer service in the chapel. Classes were held in the morning and again after midday dinner. Evening prayer, or evensong, was said at five o'clock. A light supper followed, and the day ended when the whole student body gathered before the masters to be counted, blessed, and sent to bed.

The second-floor common room where the professors and masters gathered to converse and relax would today be called the faculty lounge or library. The president and masters met in the convocation room, familiarly known to generations of students as the "blue room," to conduct college business. They

Brafferton

This classroom was used by the master of the grammar school to prepare boys twelve to sixteen for college.

summoned students to the blue room to be commended or censured for their academic performance—or occasionally for their extracurricular behavior.

Built in 1732–1733, the President's House has been the residence of every president of the College of William and Mary save one: Robert Saunders, president from 1846 to 1848, remained in his home on Palace Green. Its first occupant, the Reverend James Blair, was the energetic Anglican clergyman who first induced the Virginia Assembly to favor the erection of a college and then, in 1693, persuaded King William and Queen Mary to charter and endow it. He also supervised the construction of all the early buildings and selected the first faculty and curriculum. Blair served as president for half a century.

During the last stages of the Revolution, British General Cornwallis used the house briefly as his headquarters. French officers serving under General Rochambeau occupied the house for a short time after the siege of Yorktown, causing accidental damage by fire. The French government allocated funds to repair the building.

When Robert Boyle, the noted British scientist, died in 1691, he left his personal property to charitable and pious uses at the discretion of his executors. They invested some of the funds in the manor of Brafferton in Yorkshire, England. President James Blair persuaded the executors to give most of the profits from Brafferton to the College of William and Mary to be used for the education and conversion of Indian boys.

At first, the Native American students had a classroom in the Wren Building and lodged elsewhere in the town. The Brafferton was completed for their use in 1723. Until the Revolution cut off revenue from the Boyle foundation, there were always some Indians—often a dozen or more—at the college. Most of them seem to have forgotten their prayers and their catechism after they left Williamsburg, however. So far as is known, not one of the Indians became a missionary as Boyle's executors had hoped.

The building suffered remarkably little damage over the years, although federal troops ripped its interior woodwork from the walls and used it for firewood during the Civil War. The Brafferton today houses offices for the college.

To Great Hopes Plantation

Robertson's Windmill

Brickyard

N. ENGLAND STREET

BOTETOURT STREET

Ludwell Tenement

*Tayloe House
*Tayloe Office
Tayloe Kitchen
C
D

Hay's Cabinetmaking Shop

*Peyton Randolph House

NICHOLSON

D C

Ludwell-Paradise Stable (Cooper)

Elizabeth Reynolds House

William Randolph Lodgings

SECTION

7

North England and Nicholson Back Streets

Section 7
Admission Ticket Required
Places to Shop
Other Places to Visit
Exhibition Gardens
Places to Dine
Lodging
Services or Privately Occupied

R Restrooms
C Public Telephones
D Cold Drinks
▲ Water Fountains
X Buy Tickets Here
* Original Building
♿ Accessible to Those with Disabilities

LOOKING NORTH

See Section 3
page 66

NORTH ENGLAND AND NICHOLSON BACK STREETS

An asterisk indicates that a building is an original eighteenth- or nineteenth-century structure. A blue box indicates that you need an admission ticket to see an attraction.

A mixture of buildings—substantial town houses and modest dwellings, shops and stores, lodging houses and taverns—characterized North England, Nicholson, Waller, and Francis Streets in the eighteenth century. Structures on these back streets were generally spaced farther apart than those along Duke of Gloucester Street. Working sheds, smokehouses, dairies, kitchens (some with attics or lofts for slave quarters), poultry runs, livestock pens, stables, carriage houses,

woodpiles, privies—all could be found in the backyards of the colonial capital. This was the workaday world of Williamsburg where slaves and white servants went about the drudgery of everyday life.

The dark red ■Peyton Randolph House at the corner of Nicholson and North England Streets was the home of one of the most prominent families in colonial Virginia.

The house has three parts. The oldest, which originally faced west onto North

Peyton Randolph House

England Street, was built about 1718. Sir John Randolph and his family were living there in 1724 when he bought the lot and the one-and-a-half-story house next door. In the mid-eighteenth century, the two were linked by a two-story central section that features a grand stairway and a monumental round-headed window. Inside the house is the best series of surviving paneled rooms in Williamsburg. Although most of the paneling is the usual yellow pine, the northeast room on the second floor of the oldest section is paneled completely in oak.

When he died in 1737, Sir John Randolph willed the house to his widow during her lifetime and then to his son Peyton. Sir John also left his library to Peyton, "hoping he will betake himself to the study of law." Thomas Jefferson bought the library after his cousin Peyton's death in 1775. Jefferson's library later became the nucleus of the Library of Congress. A number of Randolph's books have been identified by signature or by bookplate among the Jefferson collection there.

Peyton fulfilled his father's hopes and studied law at the Inns of Court in London. He was appointed attorney general of the colony of Virginia in 1744, elected to the House of Burgesses in 1748, became Speaker of the House in 1766, and presided over it at every session in the crucial decade before the Revolution. In 1774, he traveled to Philadelphia where he was elected unanimously to be president of the first Continental Congress.

In August 1774, just before the Continental Congress convened, legislators met at the Peyton Randolph House to determine what course Virginia's delegates should follow. Thomas Jefferson was ill and could not attend, but he sent his suggestions to his cousin Peyton and they were read aloud to a group of patriots. Jefferson's document was soon printed and distributed as *A Summary View of the Rights of British America*. Too radical for some but moving to all, it was one of the influential tracts that led colonial Americans toward independence.

Mrs. Betty Harrison Randolph continued to live in the house after her husband's death. She relinquished it for a time during the War

MEET . . . THE RANDOLPH FAMILY

The Randolphs were the first family of Williamsburg during the colonial period. Considered the most distinguished lawyer in the colony, Sir John Randolph (1693–1737) was the only colonial-born Virginian to be honored with knighthood for his services to the Crown.

Sir John's sons Peyton (ca. 1721–1775) and John (1727–1784) attended the College of William and Mary, trained at the Inns of Court in London, and then practiced law. Peyton became attorney general within a year of his return to Virginia after completing his legal training in England. John succeeded his brother in that post when Peyton was elected Speaker of the House of Burgesses.

The Randolphs lived comfortably and married well. After their wedding in 1745, Peyton and his bride, Elizabeth Harrison of Berkeley plantation, resided in the house he had inherited from his father. John and Ariana Randolph lived in a handsome dwelling located at the southern end of South England Street. John and Ariana entertained in style, and their house became a popular literary and social center frequented by the colony's elite.

Although both Peyton and John were political moderates who hoped for reconciliation with the mother country, they took opposing sides in the years before the American Revolution. From the mid-1760s, John sided with the Crown. He was a close friend of governors Fauquier and Botetourt and was a confidant of Lord Dunmore. Peyton supported the colonists' cause, presiding over sessions of the first and second Continental Congresses.

John and his wife and daughters sailed "home" to England in September 1775, but his son, Edmund, remained in America. He joined the Continental army without his father's knowledge, eliciting this reaction from John: "For God's Sake return to your Family and indeed to yourself." Edmund ultimately distinguished himself in the service of Williamsburg as mayor, Virginia as attorney general and governor, and the United States: During Washington's presidency, Edmund was the first attorney general of the United States and later secretary of state.

Peyton Randolph died unexpectedly in Philadelphia of an apoplectic stroke in 1775. Embittered, John lived in England until his death in 1784, periodically petitioning Parliament to recoup the losses he incurred when he left Virginia.

for American Independence so that the comte de Rochambeau could establish his headquarters in the house before the Yorktown campaign. General Lafayette visited the house when he came to Williamsburg in 1824.

Today, the Peyton Randolph House is furnished with English and American antiques, including several pieces of Randolph family silver. Guests learn about the choices members of the household—Peyton Randolph, Betty Randolph, and their slaves—made as the colonies moved toward revolution. Sites and activities behind the house feature urban and rural activities.

In the eighteenth century, someone peering over the fence behind the Peyton Randolph House would have seen slaves bustling about, cooking and preparing food or stitching, laundering, and drying clothes and household linens. Betty Randolph, the mistress of the house, supervised them. Other slaves tended the garden or worked in the stable located toward the rear of the property.

Randolph's inventory, taken in 1776,

Robertson's Windmill

suggests that his slaves spun thread and yarn and made candles because it lists a parcel of tallow and twenty-three candle molds, five flax wheels, four reels, two spinning wheels, and parcels of wool, hemp, and flax. The inventory also includes twenty-seven slaves, some of whom may have been hired out to work elsewhere in town, a fairly common practice in the eighteenth century.

Today, the Randolph's yard is again alive with activity. Historic Trades carpenters, using eighteenth-century materials, tools, and techniques, have reconstructed the kitchen and the passageway connecting it to the main house. They have also built a smokehouse, a milk house, and several lumber houses, or storage buildings, all based on archaeological findings. Given the time of day and the season, interpreters engage in a variety of activities. Guests learn about the experience of being a household slave in a wealthy, urban household and about the many chores and tasks required to maintain the lifestyle of a family like the Randolphs.

Behind the Peyton Randolph House outbuildings is **Robertson's Windmill**, which has been reconstructed on a site owned early in the eighteenth century by William Robertson, clerk of the Council and one of early Williamsburg's leading citizens.

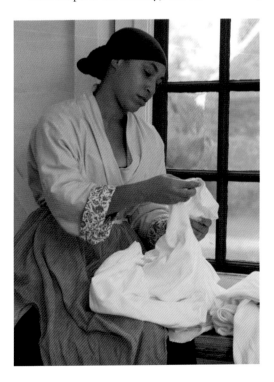

Colonial Virginians depended on local mills to grind the grain from which they made their bread, a staple of their diet that appeared at nearly every meal. Sometimes colonial householders bought cornmeal or flour for cash, or "ready money." If they brought their own grain to be ground, they might barter with the miller or agree to let him exact his time-honored one-sixth toll.

Robertson's Windmill is a post mill, so called because the whole superstructure revolves on top of a single huge post of hewed timber. The superstructure has two levels. The upper floor holds the main wind shaft and millstones; the lower floor holds the bolting, or sifting, apparatus.

The mill required constant attention to ensure that it faced the wind and that the grinding and bolting operations ran properly. If the wind changed direction, the miller lifted the stairs and pushed on the tailpole and wheel to turn the mill to face the wind.

The Windmill site also includes a field for pasturage or planting.

At ■**Great Hopes Plantation,** located off the path just beyond the windmill that

MEET . . . EVE

Eve was a slave in the household of Peyton and Betty Randolph. She worked as Betty Randolph's personal maid. In 1776 Eve was appraised at one hundred pounds, making her one of the most valuable female slaves the Randolphs owned.

Each morning, Eve laid out her mistress's clothes and helped her dress. Throughout the day, she relayed Betty's instructions to the other slaves, fetched items for her, and ran errands in Williamsburg. At night she warmed her mistress's bedsheets with a warming pan and helped Betty prepare for bed.

Eve's days were long, for she rose before her mistress and retired after Betty did. During her limited free time, Eve often took her mending to the outbuildings behind the Randolphs' house. There she would spend time with her sons, Caesar and George, while she sewed. Eve treasured these moments with her children.

Although Eve played an important role in the day-to-day activities of the Randolph household, she could not keep her family intact. After Peyton Randolph died in 1775, Betty Randolph sold fifteen-year-old Caesar. Eve's only consolation was that Caesar's new owner lived in Williamsburg, enabling her to see her older son occasionally.

Eve resolved to do everything she could to protect ten-year-old George, who was still with her. When British soldiers occupied Williamsburg in June 1781, Eve and George, now fifteen, ran away to the British forces.

In a February 1782 newspaper advertisement, Betty Randolph's nephew Harrison Randolph offered a reward "FOR apprehending EVE, Negro woman slave, who left York after the surrender . . . and has since been seen on her way to Hampton." Eve must have been captured and returned to her mistress because Betty Randolph, in a July 1782 codicil to her will, wrote that "Eve's bad behavior laid me under the necessity of selling her."

Ludwell Tenement   *Tayloe House*   *Tayloe *Office* and *Kitchen*

winds between the Visitor Center and North England Street, Colonial Williamsburg is re-creating an eighteenth-century Virginia farm. A "middling" plantation like this was very different from a huge tobacco plantation. At Great Hopes, you can experience the lives of working farmers, their families, and enslaved African Americans. Interpretations include carpentry, agriculture, and African-American enslaved life.

Skilled **carpenters** construct buildings at Great Hopes Plantation and around the Historic Area. They work from a building's foundation to its roof, planing and sawing boards, chiseling mortise and tenon joints to assemble the timber frame, raising rafters, nailing weatherboards, laying floors, constructing window sashes and doors, and making and installing stairs, moldings, and trim.

In contrast to relatively flat and straight Duke of Gloucester Street, Nicholson Street is an undulating lane that moves across a series of hills and valleys and crosses several gullies that run from the high ground of the town toward Queen's Creek and eventually to the York River. Geography affected the desirability of lots along Nicholson Street. The high ground was reserved for the few large estates in the area, leaving the cuts and washes to light industry. For example, the west end of Anthony Hay's cabinetmaking shop is built directly over a stream.

The **Ludwell Tenement,** just to the east of the Peyton Randolph House, reaffirms another

characteristic of Williamsburg's back streets: rental property and smaller houses coexisted with the homes of well-to-do residents such as the Randolphs and the Tayloes. In 1770, the Ludwell Tenement was identified as "the Tenement adjoining the Speaker," meaning the rental property next to the dwelling of Peyton Randolph, Speaker of the House of Burgesses.

The ■**Brickyard** is located behind the Tayloe House. The growth of the town in the mid-1770s sustained a concentration of carpenters, joiners, bricklayers, and plasterers. Although bricks were often made at or near building sites, brickyards like this one would have been familiar to eighteenth-century residents.

Built midway into the eighteenth century, the gambrel-roofed **Tayloe House** and property changed hands in 1759 for six hundred pounds, a very high price for a frame house at that time. One of the wealthiest men in colonial Virginia, Colonel John Tayloe, owner of the magnificent plantation called Mt. Airy in Richmond County, purchased the building probably for use as a town house. Tayloe served on the Council for many years.

The **Tayloe Office** just east of the house has an interesting "ogee," or bell-shaped, roof. This, too, is an original building.

Today, the **coopers** demonstrate their trade in the ■**Ludwell-Paradise Stable.** Usually itinerants, coopers who worked in the eighteenth-century town of Williamsburg primarily made and repaired buckets, pails, and churns.

■ *Hay's Cabinetmaking Shop*

LOOKING NORTH

Outside of town, production sites such as a mill or farm would have needed coopers to construct and repair casks for cider, grain, tobacco, and other products. Staves split from oak are formed into a circle, held in place by trussing hoops, shaped by heat, and finally given a tight-fitting head. These utilitarian products of the cooper made possible the delivery of Virginia's agricultural bounty.

■ **Hay's Cabinetmaking Shop** on the north edge of town occupied low ground between two substantial residences. On this site, a succession of cabinetmakers made some of the finest furniture in the colonies. Like many other American cabinetmakers, they also repaired furniture and musical instruments, re-silvered mirrors, and made exotic "Gothic" garden fences. They also supplied funeral services that included coffins and hearse rentals. During the Revolution, the state armorer used

The master cabinetmaker instructs his "journeyman," or assistant.

Booker Tenement

the building to repair arms for the American forces.

Anthony Hay, who had been a cabinetmaker in Williamsburg for several years, bought this lot in 1756. Hay gave up the business in 1766 when he purchased the Raleigh Tavern, after which he leased the building to former workmen. Subsequent renters of the shop included cabinetmakers Benjamin Bucktrout (who advertised that he also made and repaired spinets and harpsichords) and Edmund Dickinson (a hero of the American Revolution and probably Hay's former apprentice). Carver and gilder George Hamilton worked on this site, too.

Archaeologists found the waterlogged remains of a fence rail in the streambed under the shop. The seven-foot-long artifact showed both the crude form of the wood rail and the spacing between the pickets that had been nailed to it. The fence in front of the shop reproduces these details. Archaeological discoveries also provided evidence of clay roofing tiles like those that now cover the shop.

Many of the town's smaller households were located on Williamsburg's back streets. The **Elizabeth Reynolds House** on the south side of Nicholson Street is one of the few structures on the street that faces north.

In 1777, *Virginia Gazette* printer William Hunter deeded a narrow strip of land containing a house and garden to his mother, Elizabeth Reynolds. Hunter was illegitimate, and, although his father had acknowledged William in his will, he failed to provide for the boy's mother. Hunter's sense of duty seems to have been greater than his father's. In addition to the house and lot, he agreed to pay Elizabeth an annuity of forty pounds and to furnish a "servant maid fit and able to serve wait and attend her."

Just down the street is another example of the contrast in land use so commonplace in eighteenth-century Virginia. An unusually narrow building, the **William Randolph Lodgings** was "letten for Lodgins" in 1735 to William Randolph, the uncle of Peyton Randolph. A burgess and later a councillor, William

Elizabeth Reynolds House

William Randolph Lodgings

Coke-Garrett House

obviously considered this modest structure an appropriate residence when he came to Williamsburg on government business.

The next building on the north side of Nicholson Street, the small one-and-a-half-story **Booker Tenement,** is typical of a Williamsburg house of the "middling sort." An analysis of the tree growth ring in its timbers showed that the wood was cut about 1823. Documentary evidence indicates that Richard Booker, carpenter and town constable, had begun to rent out rooms in his newly built tenement by the spring of 1826.

■**Public Gaol.** A description of the site begins on page 73.

Facing south on Nicholson Street near its intersection with Waller Street is the **Coke-Garrett House.** In 1755, John Coke, a goldsmith and tavern keeper who already owned a house and three lots immediately to the east, bought the two lots on which the story-and-a-half west section stands. It dates from the eighteenth century. The one-and-a-half-story east section is an eighteenth-century structure that was moved to this site from an unknown location around 1837. The two-story center portion was built around 1836–1837 during the Garrett family's ownership. The brick office that served as Dr. Robert Garrett's surgery after the Battle of Williamsburg in 1862 apparently dates from about 1810. Dr. Garrett treated the wounded of both armies here.

The subdued Greek Revival architecture of the center section merges easily with the colonial styles of the east and west wings. The brick office bears full evidence of the Greek Revival style in its columned and pedimented porch.

Archaeologists found evidence of John Coke's gold- and silversmithing activities and artifacts that could be associated with a tavern on the site.

Coke left a personal estate valued at 772 pounds when he died in 1767. His widow, Sarah, continued to operate or rent out the house as a tavern. Her versatile son, Robey, repaired wagons, mounted cannon, and helved axes during the Revolution. The Garrett family acquired the property in 1810; Garretts owned it for well over a century.

Coke-Garrett dairy.

See detailed map
page 136

See Section 1
page 42

LOOKING NORTH

D U K E   O F   G L O U C E S T E R

Guardhouse

＊Magazine

S T R E E T

S T R E E T

HENRY

NASSAU

F R A N C I S   S T R E E T

PARKING

Public Hospital

Museum Store

Museum Café

The DeWitt Wallace Decorative Arts Museum and Abby Aldrich Rockefeller Folk Art Museum

PARKING

SECTION

8

Waller and Francis Back Streets

▫ Section 8		R Restrooms	
▪ Admission Ticket Required		C Public Telephones	
▫ Places to Shop		D Cold Drinks	
■ Other Places to Visit		▲ Water Fountains	
▪ Exhibition Gardens		X Buy Tickets Here	
■ Places to Dine		＊ Original Building	
▫ Lodging		♿ Accessible to Those with Disabilities	
▪ Services or Privately Occupied			

See detailed map
pages 128–129

See Section 3
page 66

See detailed map
page 122

NICHOLSON STREET

STREET

STREET

BOTETOURT STREET

Capitol

FRANCIS STREET

Ayscough House
(Gunsmith)

Presbyterian
Meetinghouse

WALLER ST.

*Benjamin Powell
House and Office

Christiana
Campbell's
Tavern

YORK ST.

*Bassett
Hall

0   100   200   300   400   500 FEET

WALLER AND FRANCIS
BACK STREETS

An asterisk indicates that a building is an original eighteenth- or nineteenth-century structure. A blue box indicates that you need an admission ticket to see an attraction.

Early in the eighteenth century, Francis and Waller Streets defined the southern and eastern limits, respectively, of the colonial capital. Town met country on the south side of Williamsburg. Slave quarters, outbuildings, barns, and fields lay immediately beyond Williamsburg's southern boundary. Then the landscape stretched away into broad meadows and wooded hillsides.

The eastern outskirts of town began to change by midcentury. Several recently built lodging houses and taverns catered to transients and townspeople who had business at the nearby Capitol. Williamsburg's second theater became a center of imported British culture, and the racetrack just east of town drew large crowds. As Williamsburg grew, a shortage of residential space in this area spurred the development of subdivisions at the east end of town and along Francis Street. A number of local tradesmen took advantage of the opportunity to buy small lots at attractive prices. An artisan could build a dwelling and perhaps open a shop here.

L A F A Y E T T E   S T R E E T

0   100   200   300 FEET

N I C H O L S O N   S T R E E T

W A L L E R   S T R E E T

*Benjamin Powell House
and Office

Elizabeth Carlos House

Christiana
Campbell's
Tavern

PARKING

PARKING

Presbyterian
Meetinghouse

Isham Goddin Shop

David
Morton
Shop and
House

George Jackson
House
and Store

Cogar
Shop

*Robert Nicolson
House

George
Davenport
House

Y O R K   S T R E E T

Capitol

F R A N C I S   S T .

*Benjamin Waller
House

LOOKING
NORTH

*Bassett Hall

PARKING

Benjamin Powell House   *Benjamin Powell Office*   Elizabeth Carlos House

The ■**Benjamin Powell House** is named for a successful builder who obtained the property in 1763. Powell sold the property in 1782, and it changed hands several times before Benjamin Carter Waller, the son of an early owner, bought it in 1794. The small brick building next to the restored house probably served as the office of Waller's son, Dr. Robert Waller, to whom he deeded that part of the property in 1814. The temple-style brick office is similar to the one at the Coke-Garrett House across the street. Today, the Benjamin Powell House is open seasonally to school groups and other guests.

In 1772, Elizabeth Carlos bought the lot on which a story-and-a-half frame house now stands. Typical of Williamsburg's more modest dwellings, the dusky brown color of

MEET . . . BENJAMIN POWELL

From a modest background as, probably, the son of a middling planter family, Benjamin Powell began his working life as a wheelwright, carpenter, and joiner. This up-and-coming businessman became a major contractor (or "undertaker," as contractors were then called) who worked on a number of Williamsburg landmarks. Powell repaired the Public Gaol in 1765, built the tower at Bruton Parish Church in 1769, repaired the Capitol in 1769 and the Palace in 1771, built the Public Hospital in 1771, and worked on soldiers' barracks in 1776. Powell was also a large landowner in nearby James City and York Counties and owner of numerous slaves.

Powell's public service included serving as a petit juror in the 1750s, a grand juror in the 1760s, and a justice of the county court in the 1770s. In 1767, he became a member of Williamsburg's Common Council, the city's municipal government. In 1770, he became keeper of the keys to the Capitol. In 1774 and 1775, he served with Peyton Randolph and George Wythe on the Committee of Safety. The committee enforced an embargo of selected British goods in 1774 and, after Lord Dunmore fled the city, took over many government functions.

Benjamin Powell's upward mobility extended to his daughters, Hannah and Nancy. Hannah married William Drew, who served as clerk of the Virginia Senate, and Nancy married John Burwell, a member of the powerful Burwell and Blair families.

the reconstructed **Elizabeth Carlos House** would have been familiar to early residents, since not every house in town was painted white.

A manuscript account book records purchases of gloves, hose, ribbons, thread, and fabric from Mrs. Carlos in 1777 and indicates that she made aprons and gowns. This evidence suggests that Elizabeth Carlos was a milliner and dressmaker who carried on her business in her home.

Christiana Campbell announced in October 1771 that she had opened a "Tavern in the House, behind the Capitol," where she promised "genteel Accommodations, and the very best Entertainment," by which she meant food and drink. A distinguished clientele patronized Mrs. Campbell's. When George Washington came to town to attend the House of Burgesses in the spring of 1772, he recorded in his diary that he dined there ten times within two months. Washington and his friends often gathered at **Christiana Campbell's Tavern** for refreshments and discussions of everything from horse races to politics.

Today, Christiana Campbell's Tavern is the area's premiere seafood restaurant. Charming balladeers entertain guests as they are invited to dine on regional favorites in the tavern that was George Washington's favorite when he came to town.

Militiaman Isham Goddin acquired the small **Isham Goddin Shop** in 1778 for two hundred pounds. In 1783, he sold his plot and building for only ninety pounds, a decrease

George Jackson House and *Store*

that reflects both wartime inflation and the collapse of Williamsburg property values after the capital moved to Richmond in 1780. The shop now serves as a hotel accommodation.

In 1777, tailor David Morton purchased the lot on the corner of Waller and York Streets for four hundred pounds, a sum that indicates the transaction included the **David Morton House** and **Shop** and the shop next door, which Morton sold to Isham Goddin the next year. Morton, an active member of the Williamsburg Lodge of Masons, served as treasurer of the lodge from 1780 to 1786. Today, his house is a hotel facility.

The **George Jackson House** and **Store** on York Street was once owned by a patriotic merchant who risked his life as well as his fortune during the Revolutionary War. Jackson chartered a ship, sailed it to Bermuda, and returned with a supply of much-needed gunpowder for the American forces.

Jackson acquired the property shortly after he moved to Williamsburg from Norfolk in 1773 or 1774. The different roof slopes indicate that this building was, in effect, two

Christiana Campbell's Tavern

Isham Goddin Shop

Cogar Shop

LOOKING NORTH

*Robert Nicolson House

buildings. The window and door arrangements of the east wing are typical of shops in the eighteenth century, and the rear chimney would have heated a small counting room. Jackson probably used this part of the structure as his store. The property now serves as hotel accommodations.

The **Cogar Shop,** a small eighteenth-century building, was moved from King and Queen County to this lot in 1947. Colonial Williamsburg later acquired this property.

Robert Nicolson, a tailor and merchant, built the last structure on York Street, the gambrel-roofed **Robert Nicolson House,** about midcentury. The off-center entrance door testifies to two periods of construction, the eastern part possibly as early as 1752 and the western part a little later. For several years thereafter, Nicolson took in lodgers.

Nicolson initially had his shop across the street. When his eldest son, William, joined him in the tailoring business in 1774, they opened a shop and store on Duke of Gloucester Street, a much better location for commercial purposes. During the Revolution,

Nicolson served on the local committee of safety. He and William provided uniforms to the American army.

■**Bassett Hall.** A description of the site begins on page 147.

Benjamin Waller acquired the property on which the **Benjamin Waller House** is located before 1750, and it remained in the Waller family for over a century. A prominent Williamsburg attorney, Waller was George Wythe's law teacher. He held a variety of offices during an impressive career: burgess, city recorder, judge of the Court of Admiralty, and vestryman of Bruton Parish.

Waller probably used the office, which is adjacent to the house on the east, in his law practice. The smokehouse is an original structure. Behind the Benjamin Waller House is a formal garden. It has been re-created with the help of a sketch drawn in the early 1800s.

Like most old houses, this house is the product of several building phases. The earliest portion is the single large room to the left of the front door. Later on, a center stair passage and then a large formal room for

David Morton Shop **and** *House*

Benjamin Waller House

entertaining were added to the west end, followed by a gambrel-roofed extension in the rear.

The horizontal weatherboards, some of them original, on the dormer cheeks are unusual because such boards are generally attached at an angle that matches the roof slope. The ornamental fence pickets at the east end of the yard are copied from a surviving eighteenth-century specimen that had been used in reroofing the house during the nineteenth century.

MEET . . . JAMES INNES

To win the Revolution, America needed not only generals like George Washington but also largely unknown leaders like James Innes.

As a student at the College of William and Mary, Innes knew well many future Revolutionary leaders. Like Thomas Jefferson, he was a member of a group called the F.H.C. Society, which came to be known as the Flat Hat Club, though, as with most fraternities, it more likely stood for something Latin, perhaps *Fraternitas Hilaritas Cognitioque*. Even as a student, Innes was a Revolutionary; he wrote a series of articles in the *Virginia Gazette* criticizing Great Britain's treatment of the colonies.

Innes's military career began in the spring of 1775 when, amid rising tension between the colonists and the governor Lord Dunmore, he organized and led one of several volunteer companies in Williamsburg, partly recruited from among students at the college. After an incident in early June 1775 at the Magazine in which three young men were wounded, the House of Burgesses officially requested Innes and his men to remain on guard there, an act that Dunmore interpreted as an attempt to usurp his executive authority. In the fall, Innes, by then a major, led his volunteers to Hampton to patrol the lower peninsula against British raids. Innes fought in numerous battles, most notably rallying American troops at Germantown in Pennsylvania. Back in Virginia in 1778, Innes served as president of the Board of War and led militia forces after the British invaded in 1781.

At the Virginia Convention of 1788, Innes, then Virginia's attorney general, spoke eloquently on behalf of adopting the federal constitution. In doing so, he managed to counteract the words of America's most admired orator, Patrick Henry, who opposed the constitution. Henry himself described Innes's oratory as "splendid, magnificent, and sufficient to shake the human mind."

Innes married Elizabeth Cocke of Williamsburg, and the couple had two children.

George Davenport House

The **George Davenport House** across the street once belonged to attorney George Davenport, whose descendants owned the property until 1779. In 1780, John Draper, a blacksmith who had come to Virginia with governor Lord Botetourt in 1768, bought the property. Draper operated a blacksmith and farrier business on Duke of Gloucester Street.

On June 17, 1765, a group of local residents successfully petitioned York County Court "for occasional Worship" at a house "Situate on a part of a Lott belonging to Mr. George Davenport as a place for Public Worship of God according to the Practise of Protestant Dissenters of the Presbyterian denomination."

The seventeen men who signed the petition were mostly Williamsburg tradesmen including a carpenter/joiner, a blacksmith, a hatter, a printer/bookbinder, a staymaker, a cabinetmaker, a wheelwright, two shoemakers, and two tailors. Two were former assistants to the keeper of the Public Gaol, and several served regularly as petit jurors in the county court. Solid members of Williamsburg society, they dissented from the established Church of England to worship as Presbyterians in staunchly Anglican Williamsburg.

Today, the ■**Presbyterian Meetinghouse** is in the George Davenport Stable—the large building behind the George Davenport House. The stable has been reinterpreted to represent the kind of space used by this group.

The **James Moir House** and **James Moir Shop** are named for the tailor who owned

this property from 1777 to about 1800 and operated his business on the site.

In an effort to supplement his income, Moir opened his home to lodgers. In 1784, when Walker Maury, a 1775 graduate of the College of William and Mary, established a grammar school in the old Capitol, Moir advertised that he had "furnished his house to accommodate eight or ten [pupils] with the greatest degree of conveniency." Moir offered "to lodge, board, wash and mend for them, at a very low price."

■**Ayscough House** (Gunsmith). A description of the site appears on page 75.

In a letter written in 1809, St. George Tucker called the **William Finnie House** on the south side of Francis Street "the handsomest house in town." It is a precursor of the classicism that began to change the American architectural scene after the Revolution. From the 1770s to the mid-1780s, William Finnie and his family lived here. During the American Revolution, Finnie served as quartermaster general of the Southern Department.

James Semple, a judge and professor of law at the college, acquired the property in 1800 and insured the house and all its outbuildings for two thousand dollars. A sketch of the front of the building drawn on the insurance declaration documents provides evidence that the house looked then just as it does today. The William Finnie House is depicted on the Frenchman's Map of 1782. The **William Finnie Quarters,** the small building just east of the house, is also an original structure.

In the eighteenth century, several lots—now

See Section 1, page 42

FRANCIS

ℬecoming ᴀmericans
Our Struggle to Be Both Free and Equal

RELIGION IN VIRGINIA

Imagine an age in which religion permeated everyday life and learning; a society in which the law sent people to court if they failed to attend the Church of England and required Quakers, Presbyterians, Baptists, and other non-Anglicans to register with the authorities; a system that empowered parish vestries to tax people of all religions to pay for poor relief, Anglican ministers' salaries, and repairs to Anglican churches such as Bruton Parish Church in Williamsburg. But think also of a clash of cultures in which Native Americans resisted English colonists' attempts at conversion and many slaves learned more than obedience from Christianity.

In the wake of the religious revivals known as the Great Awakening, many Virginians—black and white, rich and poor—sought spiritual renewal among evangelical Presbyterians and Baptists. The Presbyterian Meetinghouse near the Capitol and the African American Religion Exhibit on Nassau Street tell the stories of Presbyterians and Baptists in Williamsburg. These "New Lights," as they were called, increasingly ignored legal restraints on dissenters and pressured legislators to abolish Virginia's state church. Meanwhile, "enlightened" views gained from the study of history, philosophy, science, and religion led Thomas Jefferson, James Madison, and other Revolutionary leaders to insist that free exercise of religion be among the rights they would go to war to secure.

James Moir House

James Moir Shop

vacant—along Francis Street combined with property south of the town's boundary to form urban estates. The people who lived here often described their residences as being "pleasantly situated."

Constructed in 1695, the **Nelson-Galt House** on the north side of Francis Street is the oldest dwelling in town and among the oldest frame houses in Virginia. William Robertson, clerk of the Council, bought the property and

remodeled the house about 1709.

Thomas Nelson, a member of a prominent Yorktown family, owned the house later in the century. General Nelson, who signed the Declaration of Independence, commanded Virginia's forces during the Yorktown campaign and succeeded Thomas Jefferson as governor of the Commonwealth of Virginia.

Dr. Alexander Dickie Galt, visiting physician at the Public Hospital, purchased the

William Finnie Quarters

William Finnie House

Shields Stable

*Nelson-Galt House

house in 1823. Descendants of the Galt family, residents of Williamsburg since colonial days, continued to live here until recently.

The small **Nelson-Galt Office** nearby is also original. In the eighteenth century, the word "office" described any outbuilding not otherwise designated as to use.

The next structure to the west on Francis Street is an unpainted stable located at the back of the lot belonging to Shields Tavern, which fronts on Duke of Gloucester Street. The rough appearance of **Shields Stable** is probably typical of many backyard outbuildings in the colonial capital.

The elongated hip roof of the **Chiswell-Bucktrout House** is a style unusual in Williamsburg, although it was common in England at the beginning of the eighteenth century. A study of roof timbers and numbered beams in the surviving portions of the largely reconstructed dwelling established the original form of the roof.

In 1766, Colonel John Chiswell became the center of a scandal that "put the whole country into a ferment." Accused of killing Robert Rutledge during a tavern brawl,

Colonel Chiswell was arrested for murder. As was customary in such cases, bail was refused, but three of the colonel's friends, who were also judges of the General Court, reversed the decision and released Chiswell on bail. The less privileged attributed this unusually lenient procedure to the colonel's political and family connections. The colonel died the day before his trial—by his own hand, it was rumored.

Cabinetmaker Benjamin Bucktrout resided and worked here by the 1770s. Today, the Chiswell-Bucktrout House and its freestanding kitchen are hotel facilities.

The **Ewing House** is named for Ebenezer Ewing, a Scottish merchant. When he died in 1795, Ewing left the house to Elizabeth Ashton, the mother of his illegitimate son Thomas, with the proviso that "the moment she marries . . . it becomes the property of my son." Elizabeth remained single until her death four years later, when young Thomas inherited the dwelling. In 1805, the Williamsburg Hustings Court ordered the boy's legal guardian "to bond out Thomas Ewing for three years to learn the art of seaman or mariner"; Thomas

Chiswell-Bucktrout House

Nelson-Galt Kitchen and *Office

disappeared before completing his apprenticeship. The Ewing House and Shop are now hotel accommodations.

Josias Moody, a blacksmith, owned the unpretentious house next door from 1794 until he died about 1810. Architectural evidence suggests that the **Moody House** dates from 1725 to 1750. The house was altered several times before reaching its present size and appearance by 1782. The long lean-to roof on the back indicates that additions were made to an earlier structure. The kitchen behind the house is now a hotel facility.

The **Dr. Barraud House** on the northwest corner of Francis and Botetourt Streets was erected before 1782 and incorporated an earlier building on the site. Dr. Philip Barraud, the buyer in 1786, was born in Virginia, saw active service during the Revolution, studied medicine at the University of Edinburgh, and, with Dr. John Minson Galt, served as visiting physician to the Public Hospital until he moved to Norfolk in 1799.

The Dr. Barraud House is one of the few residences that front Francis Street on the north. For the most part, the north side of

*Ewing House

MEET . . .
GOWAN PAMPHLET

Gowan Pamphlet followed a path few would have imagined possible for an enslaved person. Hemmed in by law, custom, fear, and prejudice, he managed to preach a message of equality before God to a congregation of black people.

Pamphlet began preaching in the 1770s after Moses, an itinerant black preacher, left Williamsburg. At the time, Pamphlet was the property of Jane Vobe, owner of the King's Arms Tavern, and to carry out his ministry he had to negotiate time away from his duties at the tavern. Preaching was extremely risky since authorities were quick to associate slave religion with rebellion and the law allowed patrols to lash anyone caught meeting secretly.

Oral tradition suggests that Pamphlet first preached hidden in arbors made of saplings and underbrush at Green Spring plantation, several miles from town. Undaunted by threats, black people flocked to hear him preach and to be baptized under his hand. By 1781, the congregation numbered two hundred and may have begun gathering in a wooded area on the outskirts of Williamsburg.

In 1793, there was talk that the enslaved pastor was a messenger for a network of armed slaves. That same year, for reasons we don't know, Pamphlet's then-owner, David Miller, drew up a deed that would set him free. Also in 1793, amid gradually increasing but by no means universal acceptance of black people's Christianity, Pamphlet attended the annual meeting of a regional association of white Baptist churches during which his church was accepted for membership. Later, the congregation held services in a wooden carriage house on Nassau Street where today there is a historical marker and exhibit.

Masonic Lodge

Masonic Kitchen

Francis Street gives access to the back of Duke of Gloucester Street lots, where stables, privies, and other outbuildings were usually located in the eighteenth century.

The **Lewis House** is named for Charles Lewis who owned the property until 1806 and is believed to have built the original house. Initially the lot was part of the Orlando Jones property, which extended from Duke of Gloucester Street to Francis Street. Hotel guests can now stay in the house.

Probably built between 1750 and 1775, the **Orrell House** takes its name from John Orrell, who acquired the property about 1810.

The entrance hall, or "passage," of the house, an otherwise typical gambrel-roofed dwelling, is not centered, so all the living quarters are to one side of the passage. The house forms on plan an exact square whose sides measure twenty-eight feet, and, because the roof ridge is twenty-eight feet above the top of the basement wall, it is proportioned as an ideal geometric cube. Today, it is a hotel facility.

The **Quarter,** a small nineteenth-century cottage, is believed to have served for a time as slave quarters. The addition of a shed portion at the rear of the building has resulted in an unusual and attractive roofline. The Quarter is now a hotel facility.

The **Richard Crump House** is named for its late-eighteenth-century owner. The Reverend Mr. John Bracken, who had extensive real estate holdings along Francis Street, owned the house briefly along with the **Bracken Tenement** to the west and the **Bracken Kitchen,** which is located between the two dwellings. Hotel guests can stay in the Richard Crump House or the Bracken Kitchen.

Bracken's rise to social and financial prominence began in 1776 with his marriage to Sally Burwell of Carter's Grove plantation. He was the rector of Bruton Parish Church for forty-five years, mayor of Williamsburg in 1796, and president of the College of William and Mary from 1812 to 1814.

As the rector grew older, he became rotund and perhaps overfond of the grape. In 1815, one observer recounted how Bracken kept a couple waiting at the altar. Apparently the

*Moody House

*Orrell House

Lewis House

*Dr. Barraud House

"Round Bellied Vicar" imbibed a drop too much en route to Yorktown to conduct the wedding. He lost his way, "upset the jigg and broke it," and arrived—wet and muddy—an hour late for the ceremony.

The one-and-a-half-story Bracken Tenement has a steep A-shaped gable roof and massive T-shaped chimneys, each characteristic of early-eighteenth-century architecture in Virginia.

The **Masonic Kitchen** and **Masonic Lodge** on the north side of Francis Street stand where "the ancient and loyal society of free and accepted Masons" met in the late eighteenth century. The Williamsburg chapter, which had been meeting at local taverns since midcentury, received a new charter in 1773. Its members included Peyton Randolph, Peter Pelham, Bishop James Madison, St. George Tucker, and James Monroe.

In the 1770s, the lodge held its regular meetings at Market Square Tavern and patronized Christiana Campbell's Tavern for balls and special entertainments. The Masons leased a portion of this lot and met in a building on

this property from the 1780s onward. Today, the Masonic Kitchen is a hotel facility.

Architectural evidence suggests that the **Lightfoot House,** built about 1730, was brought to its final form in the 1750s. This fine brick residence is unusual in having a second floor as high as the first. It is adorned by a stringcourse in molded brick and by a wrought-iron balcony suggestive of the one at the Governor's Palace. The decorative front fence shows the Chinese, or chinoiserie, influence so popular about 1750.

The Lightfoot family owned this property during much of the eighteenth century. In 1783, Philip Lightfoot advertised the house for sale, describing it as "a large two story brick dwelling house, with four rooms on a floor; its situation is esteemed one of the most pleasant in the City, lying on the back-street near the market." The Reverend John Bracken bought the property in 1786.

The Lightfoot House has been furnished with fine antiques and is equipped with modern conveniences to serve as an appropriate guesthouse for distinguished guests of Colonial

*The Quarter   Richard Crump House   Bracken Kitchen   *Bracken Tenement

The handsome brick Lightfoot House provides accommodations for VIPs to Williamsburg. The style of the chinoiserie front fence was fashionable about 1750.

Williamsburg. The laundry and kitchen behind it serve as hotel accommodations.

The Reverend Mr. Bracken also bought the **Lightfoot Tenement** next door. In the eighteenth century, the term "tenement" meant simply a rented house. The Lightfoot Tenement is now a hotel facility.

All that remains on the site of the Nicholas-Tyler House on the southwest corner of South England Street are two buildings. The **Nicholas-Tyler Office** and **Nicholas-Tyler**

Laundry have been reconstructed on their original foundations. The structures are hotel accommodations.

Robert Carter Nicholas bought the property in 1770 and built a large frame house with numerous outbuildings. Nicholas served as treasurer of the colony of Virginia and later as a judge of the Chancery Court.

A later owner was John Tyler, tenth president of the United States. Tyler and his family were living here when two horsemen reined up in front of the house early on April 5, 1841. They knocked on the door and waited. John Tyler, clad in a nightshirt and cap, finally

*Lightfoot House

Lightfoot Tenement*

The Lightfoot Tenement garden.

opened the door, only to learn that President William Henry Harrison had died and the awesome duties of the presidency now rested on his shoulders.

Near the west end of Francis Street, standing alone on the south side of the street is the **Custis Kitchen.** It marks the eight lots owned by Colonel John Custis—scholar, planter, and eccentric—who settled in Williamsburg about 1715.

Here Custis built a substantial brick house and a number of outbuildings and cultivated his celebrated garden, one of the most ambitious ornamental and experimental gardens in early America. Correspondence that records Custis's exchange of plant specimens with the great English natural history enthusiast Peter Collinson has been helpful in planting the gardens of Colonial Williamsburg's Historic Area.

When Custis died in 1749, his son, Daniel Parke Custis, inherited Custis Square. Daniel's widow, Martha, subsequently married George Washington, who administered the property until his stepson, John Parke ("Jacky") Custis, came of age in 1778.

Francis Fauquier, one of the colony's most popular royal governors, first proposed the

Nicholas-Tyler Office

Nicholas-Tyler Laundry

The map shows:

STREET (left side, vertical) · STREET (right side, vertical, labeled NASSAU going down)

*Travis House

STREET

FRANCIS ST.

HENRY (vertical)

NASSAU (vertical)

*Custis Kitchen

R &
C ▲

Public Hospital

The DeWitt Wallace Decorative Arts Museum
and Abby Aldrich Rockefeller Folk Art Museum

Museum Store

Museum Café   X

PARKING

establishment of the ■**Public Hospital** to the House of Burgesses in 1766. Until that time, the insane in Virginia were cared for at home, maintained in a neighbor's house in exchange for money from tax revenues collected by church vestries for poor relief, or confined with vagrants in parish workhouses. Some were even incarcerated in the Williamsburg Public Gaol.

The General Assembly enacted legislation "to make Provision for the support and maintenance of idiots, lunatics, and other persons of unsound Minds" in 1770. The Public Hospital, the first public institution in British North America devoted exclusively to the care and treatment of the mentally ill, opened in 1773. Well-known Philadelphia architect Robert Smith designed the building. George Wythe, John Blair, and Thomas Nelson were among its original trustees.

The Public Hospital continued to minister to the mentally ill of the Commonwealth of Virginia until a disastrous fire swept through the facility in 1885 and destroyed the colonial building. The hospital was rebuilt on this site, where it remained until Eastern State Hospital on the outskirts of Williamsburg opened in the mid-1960s.

The Public Hospital was the last major public building of eighteenth-century Williamsburg to be reconstructed. The reconstruction follows the form and details of the original building, which were determined by archaeological investigations and historical research. Exhibitions show how the treatment of mental illness evolved in the eighteenth

LOOKING SOUTH

Custis Kitchen

Travis House

and nineteenth centuries. An underground concourse connects the hospital with the contemporary, two-level DeWitt Wallace Decorative Arts Museum and the Abby Aldrich Rockefeller Folk Art Museum.

■**The DeWitt Wallace Decorative Arts Museum.** A description of the museum begins on page 141.

■**Abby Aldrich Rockefeller Folk Art Museum.** A description of the museum begins on page 144.

On the north side of Francis Street is the

Travis House, a long, gambrel-roofed frame structure. Colonel Edward Champion Travis, a member of the House of Burgesses, erected the western portion of this dwelling before 1765; later residents added on to the house over the next half century until it reached its present seventy-foot length. The additions are marked today by the vertical boards that originally were the corner boards of their respective sections. Superintendents of the Public Hospital lived in the Travis House until early in the twentieth century.

■ *Public Hospital*

▪PUBLIC HOSPITAL

"Every civilized Country has an Hospital for these People, where they are confined, maintained and attended by able Physicians, to endeavour to restore to them their lost reason."

Governor Francis Fauquier presented this rationale in 1766 when he first proposed that a hospital be founded to care "for these miserable Objects, who cannot help themselves." On June 4, 1770, the House of Burgesses passed a bill to establish the Public Hospital, which opened in the fall of 1773 as the first public institution in the British North American colonies devoted solely to the care and treatment of the mentally ill.

Over the next eleven decades, the Public Hospital grew into a complex of nine buildings. As the physical appearance of the hospital changed, so too did the ways in which mental illness was regarded and treated.

During the period 1773–1835, the hospital was part prison, part infirmary. Its first keeper, James Galt, had formerly been in charge of the Public Gaol. His wife, Mary, became the matron for the female patients. Dr. John de

The interior of a patient's room or cell as it would have appeared in the Public Hospital during the late eighteenth century.

Sequeyra, a physician educated in Holland, served as the attending doctor from 1773 to 1795. He saw patients when they were admitted and once a week thereafter. A court of directors drawn from Virginia's gentry class determined admissions, ordered discharges, and made policy decisions. Only those considered dangerous or curable were admitted.

Physicians in this "Age of Restraint" regarded mental illness as a disease of the brain, and the belief that mentally disturbed people could be cured by using scientific knowledge was relatively new. To calm or cure patients, the staff applied mechanical restraints, prescribed potent drugs, employed the ducking chair or plunge bath, and used instruments to bleed them.

The "Moral Management Era," 1836–1862, saw a new approach to mental health care. Moral management deemphasized restraints and stressed the importance of kindness in efforts to cure the mentally ill. Physical labor, organized leisure-time activities, and careful medical supervision were also important aspects of everyday life in the Public Hospital during this period. Patients were urged to participate in crafts, gardening, and musical diversions and to talk with one another and with the staff.

The Public Hospital's physical facilities and patient population grew dramatically by the mid-nineteenth century. A third floor was added to the original structure and other buildings were enlarged. By 1859, the Public

Hospital housed three hundred patients in seven buildings.

Although the Public Hospital had grown in size by the late nineteenth century, the percentage of patients successfully treated declined drastically. The staff lost confidence in their ability to cure mental illness, and, without a clear sense of direction, the facility became a long-term home for the chronically ill. The Public Hospital had entered its third phase, the "Custodial Care Regime," 1862–1885.

Physical restraints appeared, and a maintenance program of passive diversions such as magic lantern shows, fishing excursions, picnics, and tea parties was instituted. The number of patients rose to more than 440 by 1883, and it became clear that the authorities had decided simply to care for the mentally disturbed without initiating a course of treatment that might result in a cure.

On the night of June 7, 1885, a fire of undetermined origin completely destroyed the eighteenth-century Public Hospital building, which was reconstructed by the Colonial Williamsburg Foundation in 1985.

The exhibition in the east wing of the reconstructed Public Hospital has two parts. From the central hall, guests enter the east passage, a reconstructed historical space that contained six of the twenty-four cells found in the original building. On the north side of the passage is a central viewing room. From this modern vantage point, guests can look into a re-created eighteenth-century cell, a cold and spare prisonlike interior with chains on the wall and bars at the window. Opposite is a mid-nineteenth-century apartment, a more comfortable environment in which patients were encouraged to communicate with other patients and with the staff. The exhibition cells highlight the changes in treatments and doctor-patient relationships between the eighteenth and nineteenth centuries.

The modern exhibition area on the south side of the building contains a three-part display that graphically shows the different theories about mental illness and methods of treating it that were in fashion from the opening of the Public Hospital until the devastating fire in 1885.

The interior of a patient's apartment as it would have appeared at the Williamsburg asylum during the mid-1840s.

THE DEWITT WALLACE DECORATIVE ARTS MUSEUM

A bi-level contemporary museum, the DeWitt Wallace Decorative Arts Museum is contained within a high brick wall immediately behind the reconstructed Public Hospital. The museum is entered through the hospital lobby at the lower level. Completed in 1985 with funds provided by the late De-Witt and Lila Acheson Wallace, founders of *Reader's Digest*, the museum is devoted to the exhibition and interpretation of a broad range of primarily British and American decorative

Philadelphia chest on chest.

George Washington *by Charles Willson Peale.*

arts. Dating from the seventeenth century to the early nineteenth century, these examples include furniture, ceramics, silver and base metals, paintings, prints, textiles and costumes, and many other domestic objects from Colonial Williamsburg's collections.

Designed by internationally honored architect Kevin Roche, the museum is contemporary in concept and versatile in function and presentation. The main floor is penetrated by a glass-roofed garden court that allows controlled sunlight to illuminate the adjacent galleries. A handsome stairway draws guests

The museum's rich collections are featured in innovative exhibitions.

in styles and techniques as they view greater quantities of objects that span a broader range of aesthetic and technical accomplishment.

In a wide variety of ways, the objects in these galleries—some of which probably might not have come to Williamsburg because of a variety of factors—help guests better understand how colonial Virginians, many of whom were transplanted Englishmen and women or their descendants, became Americans. With advance notice, guided tours of the DeWitt Wallace Decorative Arts Museum are offered to complement and enhance guest experiences in the Historic Area.

Special lectures, musical events, craft programs, and video presentations are offered (according to a published schedule) in a 240-seat auditorium named for June S. and Joseph H. Hennage. Decorative arts publications as well as reproductions of some of the objects exhibited in the gallery may be purchased in the museum shop adjoining the lower lobby. Luncheon, tea, and other light refreshments are available in the museum's café on the lower level beside the central court.

through the lower-level Introductory Gallery and leads them up to the main, or ground, level, where the primary exhibition areas are located.

Several different gallery spaces occupy the main level. They include individual media study galleries and galleries for special exhibitions. An array of objects that are important historically and aesthetically to the study of the colonial period are displayed around the balcony that overlooks the garden court.

Exhibition space on either side of the center area is devoted to a series of study galleries where British and American textiles, maps and prints, metals, and furniture are permanently displayed. Ceramics are exhibited in an innovative display called "Revolution in Taste." In these more intimate spaces, museum guests can quietly study and absorb subtle differences

The superb tall case clock has works by Thomas Tompion.

ABOVE: *A stunning display of eighteenth-
and early-nineteenth-century silver is on
view in the Mary Jewett Gaiser Silver
Gallery.* LEFT: *Silver soup tureen by George
Wickes.* RIGHT: *"Mr. Nobody," delft.*

■ABBY ALDRICH ROCKEFELLER FOLK ART MUSEUM

*A*merican folk art is the product of talented but minimally trained or untrained artists and craftspeople working outside the mainstream of academic art. Since colonial times, America's untutored artists have recorded aspects of everyday life, making novel and effective use of whatever media are at hand. Bold colors, simplified shapes, imaginative surface patterns, and the artist's highly original and unselfconscious use of various media are characteristics of the best objects created by amateurs and artisans.

Among the objects on view at the Abby Aldrich Rockefeller Folk Art Museum are pictures done in oil, watercolor, ink, and needlework that describe a variety of subjects, such as portraits; land- and seascapes; scenes of daily life; biblical, historical, and literary pieces; still lifes; fraktur; and family records. Three-dimensional carvings or sculpture executed in wood and metal include weather vanes and wind toys, ship carvings, shop signs, toys, and decoys. Among household furnishings are boxes, woven and quilted bed coverings, pottery, tinware, iron utensils, and furniture embellished with painted decoration. Objects date from the eighteenth century to the present.

American quilts, such as these nineteenth-century examples, and woven bed coverlets are rotated on display in the Foster and Muriel McCarl Textile Gallery.

The family-friendly "Down on the Farm" exhibit.

Abby Aldrich Rockefeller pioneered in collecting American folk art in the late 1920s at a time when others ignored its aesthetic appeal and often considered the material curious, quaint, or worth saving only because of its historical associations. Mrs. Rockefeller sought out and acquired more than four hundred pieces of folk art during a ten-year period. In 1935, she loaned the principal part of her collection to the Colonial Williamsburg Foundation, and, in 1939, the loan became a gift. A folk art museum, built in her memory by her husband, John D. Rockefeller Jr., opened to the public in 1957. Since then, the collection has expanded to more than four thousand objects.

In 2005–2006, the museum relocated to an updated and expanded facility adjacent to the DeWitt Wallace Decorative Arts Museum. The new building offers changing exhibitions of American folk art as well as exciting new displays of the permanent collection.

Coach by unidentified maker, circa 1900.

▪BASSETT HALL

At the east end of Francis Street, guests will find Bassett Hall, the Williamsburg home of Abby Aldrich and John D. Rockefeller Jr. The Rockefellers acquired Bassett Hall in October 1927, although it was several years before they took up residence. Mrs. Rockefeller was especially pleased by the prospect of a home in Williamsburg. She reportedly told a local resident that "John . . . says I can keep it if I promise not to take in tourists."

The Bray family owned the Bassett Hall property from the early seventeenth century until 1753 when it was transferred to Colonel Philip Johnson, husband of Elizabeth Bray. Johnson probably built the present house soon

after. The estate then consisted of 950 rural acres and four contiguous lots in the city of Williamsburg.

Richard Corbin, the next owner, refurbished the house in the 1790s. It was acquired by Burwell Bassett about 1800 and has carried the Bassett name ever since. Bassett was a Virginia legislator and the nephew of Martha Washington. Abel Parker Upshur, secretary of state under President John Tyler, owned Bassett Hall from 1840 to 1843. Subsequent owners included John Coke, Colonel Goodrich Durfey, Israel Smith and his descendants, and eventually John D. Rockefeller Jr.

A fire in 1930 destroyed part of the building's roof and stair hall and further delayed

Bassett Hall dining room.

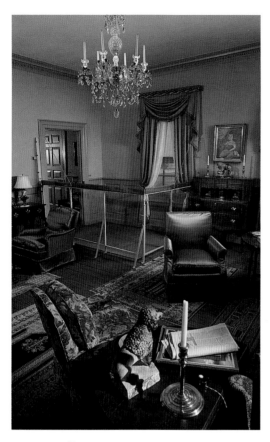

Bassett Hall morning room.

combined Continental porcelains with American figural pottery, folk paintings with portraits by studio-trained artists, and hooked rugs with Oriental carpets. The rich mixture of furnishings arranged into intimate groups gives Bassett Hall its charm. These rooms were made inviting and relaxing, an atmosphere especially appealing to Mr. Rockefeller.

The Rockefellers shared a deep interest in gardening and landscape and were closely involved in the development of Bassett Hall's extensive grounds. Near the house, they realigned the three historic outbuildings (smokehouse, kitchen, and dairy) to allow for a better view of the property. By 1938, the Rockefellers had met numerous times with Shurcliff about the design and plantings for fourteen acres of gardens, which included a large number of boxwoods. Shurcliff was also asked to design flower beds with plants that bloomed during the spring and fall when the Rockefellers were most likely to be in residence.

Mrs. Rockefeller took a special interest in the flower beds and used cuttings for floral arrangements throughout the house. An early gardening effort was the planting of wildflowers and bulbs beneath the majestic Great Oak, which stood near the edge of the south woods. Mr. Rockefeller was especially fond of the mammoth tree, which was about four hundred years old when it collapsed in 1998. He also focused much of his attention on the surrounding woodlands. With the help of Shurcliff, Mr. Rockefeller developed an allée, a walkway lined with trees, with a dramatic vista extending south from the teahouse on the west side of the house, through an avenue of oaks, and then into woods.

Mr. and Mrs. Rockefeller endeared themselves to their Williamsburg neighbors and enjoyed wide popularity in the community. During World War II, the Rockefellers supported the local USO and entertained military personnel at Bassett Hall. Afternoon teas for neighbors and dinners for community friends

the Rockefellers' renovation of the house. Colonial Williamsburg's architects were involved in the necessary repairs and restoration, but Mr. and Mrs. Rockefeller oversaw the work and also planned the interior decoration. They engaged Arthur Shurcliff, Colonial Williamsburg's landscape architect, to create a garden plan.

In furnishing Bassett Hall, the Rockefellers drew on their many interests in the arts. Mr. Rockefeller studied and collected Chinese porcelain, Oriental carpets, and European tapestries, while Mrs. Rockefeller, a founder of the Museum of Modern Art in New York, was a patron of modern American artists. From the 1920s until her death, she also formed an unprecedented collection of early American folk art. At Bassett Hall, she

Bassett Hall morning room.

and officials were also common. Mrs. Rockefeller's interest in public education led to her role in the innovative curriculum designed for Williamsburg's new Bruton Heights School, which during the era of segregation served Williamsburg's African-American children. Mr. Rockefeller gave funds for the construction of that school and the Matthew Whaley School.

Mrs. Rockefeller found Bassett Hall, the town, and her Williamsburg friends a welcome refuge from her normally hectic schedule. She once wrote, "I would like to stay on here for a month longer. It is so peaceful and quiet and the lack of excitement keeps my blood pressure from soaring to the skies."

Following Abby Aldrich Rockefeller's death in 1948, Mr. Rockefeller deeded Bassett Hall to their son John D. Rockefeller 3rd, reserving a life interest in the property. After his father's demise in 1960, John D. Rockefeller 3rd and his wife, Blanchette Hooker Rockefeller, assumed responsibility for the property. They were so impressed by the skillful arrangements of objects and charm of the interiors that they kept everything essentially as it was.

At John D. Rockefeller 3rd's death in 1978, the property was left to family members who presented it to the Colonial Williamsburg Foundation. The next year, the John D. Rockefeller 3rd Fund gave Bassett Hall furnishings to the Foundation.

A complete restoration of the Bassett Hall complex, including the gardens and historic interiors, was undertaken in 2000–2002 and generously funded by Abby O'Neill (granddaughter of Abby and John D. Rockefeller Jr.) and her husband, George O'Neill. Today, the house and grounds look much the way they did in the late 1930s and 1940s.

Bassett Hall upstairs hall.

DINING

From colonial sippets to Continental cuisine, you'll satisfy your appetite at Colonial Williamsburg's eighteenth-century taverns—Chowning's Tavern, Christiana Campbell's Tavern, the King's Arms Tavern, or Shields Tavern—where you can enjoy dishes inspired by early American recipes. Colonial politicians, the elite, and travelers gathered at taverns to partake of hearty meals, spirits, gossip, and music. Today, this atmosphere of mirth, song, and tempting aromas still prevails with costumed servers in authentically re-created dining rooms and conversation that competes with the rollicking

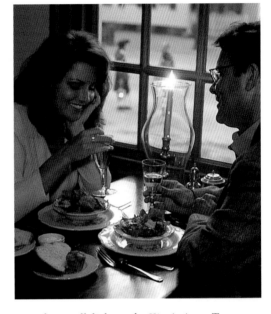

Dine by candlelight at the King's Arms Tavern.

songs of strolling balladeers. Eat at a colonial tavern for one of the most memorable dining experiences you'll ever have.

Our contemporary restaurants are equally distinctive. The award-winning Regency Room at the Williamsburg Inn offers unparalleled cuisine, elegance, and service. If you're looking for scrumptious food in a more casual atmosphere, try the Williamsburg Lodge restaurant or the Golden Horseshoe Clubhouse Grills. Enjoy pizza, sandwiches, and salads at Huzzah!, the family-style restaurant adjacent to the Williamsburg Woodlands Hotel & Suites.

What are sippets? Toasted pieces of bread you dip into soup. Once you try them, you may never go back to crackers.

CHECKLIST: GRABBING A QUICK BITE

In the Historic Area

☐ *Shields Tavern.*

☐ *Raleigh Tavern Bakery.*

☐ *Chowning's Tavern garden (open seasonally).*

☐ *King's Arms Tavern garden (open seasonally).*

☐ *Shields Tavern garden (open seasonally).*

At the Visitor Center complex

☐ *Huzzah!*

☐ *Commonwealth Coffee and Tea.*

At the DeWitt Wallace Decorative Arts Museum and Abby Aldrich Rockefeller Folk Art Museum

☐ *Museum Café.*

Visit www.colonialwilliamsburg.com/visit for restaurant details and menus.

DINING IN THE HISTORIC AREA

Casual dress is appropriate and an admission ticket is not required to dine in the following establishments. Check the monthly "Guide to Dining and Shopping" for the current schedules.

Chowning's Tavern. When Josiah Chowning opened his tavern in 1766, he promised that "all who please to favour me with their custom may depend on the best of entertainment for themselves, servants, and horses, and good pasturage." That same spirit distinguishes Chowning's Tavern today, although your horses will have to fend for themselves. Mr. Chowning's tavern attracted the ordinary sort, so modern diners will find fare like that served in eighteenth-century British alehouses. Enjoy hearty dishes such as barbecued beef brisket, grilled Smithfield sausage, oversized hickory-grilled chicken, Brunswick stew, pulled pork barbecue, brick house brownies, and cinnamon apple turnovers. A children's menu is available. Dine inside or in the garden (seasonally).

Experience eighteenth-century nightlife at Gambols, offered each evening at Chowning's Tavern. Nighttime fun can be had as balladeers lead guests in rousing sing-alongs and costumed servers lead guests in playing popular games of the day. Light food and beverages are served. Family entertainment is the rule between 5:00 and 8:00 p.m. From 8:00 p.m. until closing, Chowning's caters to a more mature audience.

Christiana Campbell's Tavern. George Washington was a faithful customer of Christiana Campbell's. In December 1762, he noted in his diary, "Mrs. Washington & children, myself, Colo. Basset, Mrs. Basset & Betcy Bassett all Eat Oysters at Mrs. Campbells." Today, Christiana Campbell's Tavern serves dishes inspired by those the Father of Our Country would have found during his travels throughout the colonies. Enjoy the friendly, informal setting while you feast on Mrs. Campbell's fried chicken, oyster fritters, crab cakes, sherried crab stew, sea pye, or black bottom chocolate pecan pie. A children's menu is available. The tavern garden is open seasonally.

CHECKLIST: FINDING MORE
LEISURELY DINING

In the Historic Area

☐ *Chowning's Tavern.*

☐ *Christiana Campbell's Tavern.*

☐ *King's Arms Tavern.*

Near the Historic Area

☐ *Golden Horseshoe Gold and Green
Course Clubhouse Grills.*

☐ *Williamsburg Inn Regency Room.*

☐ *Williamsburg Inn Restoration Bar.*

☐ *Williamsburg Lodge restaurant.*

☐ *Williamsburg Lodge lobby lounge.*

At the Visitor Center complex

☐ *Huzzah!*

*Call 1-800-HISTORY (447-8679)
to make dining reservations.*

King's Arms Tavern. After Jane Vobe opened the King's Arm Tavern in 1772, it became one of the town's most "genteel" establishments. George Washington sometimes ate here, as did Virginia's future governor Thomas Nelson Jr. General Baron von Steuben ran up a bill of nearly three hundred Spanish dollars for lodging, meals, and beverages. Present-day diners can savor traditional fare such as peanut soup, oysters, filet mignon, game pye, cavalier's lamb, roast prime rib of beef, or pecan pie. A children's menu is available. Lunch, beverages, and light fare are served in the garden. The garden is open seasonally.

Shields Tavern. In the early 1740s, James Shields took over the tavern that his father-in-law had operated several decades earlier. Shields Tavern attracted lower gentry and successful middling customers. Today, Shields Tavern operates in the tradition of an eighteenth-century coffeehouse, which archaeological research suggests existed near the Capitol. Drinks and light fare are available throughout the day. In the evening, part of the tavern operates as a bar, and light suppers are served. The tavern garden is open seasonally.

Raleigh Tavern Bakery. The smell of gingerbread baking will make your mouth water. Fortunately, you can assuage your hunger with ham biscuits, Sally Lunn bread, rolls, queen's cake, oatmeal "cakes" (cookies), and—yes—gingerbread. Quench your thirst with cider, King's Arms Tavern Ginger Ale, or Chowning's Tavern Root Beer. Enjoy a quick bite from the Bakery as you relax on a bench in the Historic Area.

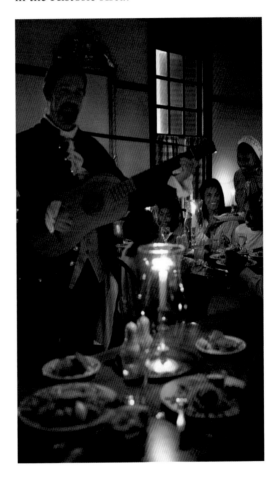

COLONIAL WILLIAMSBURG'S RESTAURANTS OUTSIDE THE HISTORIC AREA

Unless noted otherwise, casual dress is appropriate and an admission ticket is not required to dine in the following establishments. Check the monthly "Guide to Dining and Shopping" for the current schedules.

Huzzah! Contemporary families will likely cheer this fun, casual eatery conveniently located adjacent to the Williamsburg Woodlands Hotel & Suites. Featuring everyday favorites, guests can savor delicious soups, oversized burgers, salads, sandwiches, wraps, and hot made-to-order pizza and subs from our Italian-made pizza oven. Top off any meal with one of Huzzah!'s mouth-watering signature desserts. A children's menu is available for little patriots.

Golden Horseshoe Gold Course Clubhouse Grill, Golden Horseshoe Green Course Clubhouse Grill. Each of Colonial Williamsburg's championship golf courses features a clubhouse where you can enjoy both a tasty meal and a picturesque view. Choose from a delightful array of sandwiches, salads, light entrées, and desserts. Both clubhouses

have lounges that serve cocktails and other beverages.

Museum Café. Stop by the Museum Café while you are visiting the DeWitt Wallace Decorative Arts Museum or Abby Aldrich Rockefeller Folk Art Museum. The self-service café offers sandwiches, seasonal salads, soup, chili, and other luncheon fare and light refreshments, including an assortment of Colonial Williamsburg's desserts.

Williamsburg Inn Regency Room. Savor distinctive food and wines in an atmosphere of graceful elegance in the renowned Regency Room. Enjoy new American cuisine and complement your meal with the perfect wine from our wine list, named an Award of Excellence Winner by *Wine Spectator* magazine. Breakfast, afternoon tea (seasonally), and dinner are served daily. Lunch is served Monday through Saturday. Sunday brunch offers a wonderful appetizer and dessert display, scrumptious entrées carefully prepared in the kitchen, champagne, and live music—a very special occasion. Live music also accompanies dinner every evening, and dancing is offered Friday and Saturday nights. (Jacket and tie are required for dinner and jacket only for Sunday brunch in the Regency Room.)

Williamsburg Inn Restoration Bar. Enjoy cocktails and conversation at the Williamsburg Inn's intimate Restoration Bar. Commemorating the restoration of Williamsburg and the creation of the Williamsburg Inn, this clubby setting is ideal for predining gatherings and nightcaps.

Williamsburg Inn Afternoon Tea. Serving an exquisite selection of tea, this is the perfect gathering spot for traditional afternoon tea. Finger sandwiches, miniature pastries, tartlets, scones, English tea cakes, and cookies are a tempting sampling of tea accompaniments. A light fare menu is also available.

Williamsburg Lodge Restaurant. The restoration and expansion of the Williamsburg Lodge included an all-new restaurant and creative new menu selections. Prepared by an award-winning culinary team, the restaurant's cuisine is an innovative take on southern and regional favorites. A la carte and buffet options are available for breakfast and lunch and à la carte is available during dinner. The Friday night seafood buffet is a longtime favorite featuring a bountiful array of dishes served up with local flair. Sunday brunch will add the perfect touch to your day of rest. A children's menu is available.

Williamsburg Lodge Lobby Lounge. Perfect

Elegance, superior service, and outstanding food and wines are the hallmarks of the Williamsburg Inn's Regency Room.

for casual gatherings for conferees or families, the lobby lounge is a favorite relaxing spot. A beautiful fireplace, bamboo settees, and leather sofas surround the handsome bar. A light fare menu infused with southern and regional specialties along with a full selection of beverages makes for a comfortable, relaxing environment.

CHECKLIST: HOME COOKING

To enjoy colonial cuisine at home, call 1-800-446-9249 or go to www.WilliamsburgMarketplace.com to order:

☐ The Colonial Williamsburg Tavern Cookbook. *Delectable recipes, beautiful photographs, fascinating history.*

☐ Holiday Fare. *Inspired ideas for the Christmas cook, from corn pudding to hot cranberry wassail.*

☐ Recipes from the Raleigh Tavern Bakery. *Lots of goodies, with both colonial recipes and modern adaptations for the home cook.*

☐ Williamsburg Art of Cookery. *Favorite "receipts" from the eighteenth and nineteenth centuries.*

☐ The Williamsburg Cookbook. *The classic best seller.*

DINING IN MERCHANTS SQUARE

Located adjacent to the Historic Area, Merchants Square offers a range of dining experiences. Whether you want a quick bite or a four-course meal, the restaurants and specialty shops here will meet your needs. Grab a sandwich at the **Cheese Shop** or a pastry at **Steeps Tea Tavern & Elixir Bar.** Enjoy lunch or dinner—indoors or out—at **Aromas Coffee and Café, Berret's Seafood Restaurant & Taphouse Grill, Blue Talon Bistro, the Fat Canary, Pizza on the Square, Seasons Restaurant, Stephanos Pizza & Subs,** or the **Trellis Restaurant and Café.** Top off your meal with a sweet from **Baskin-Robbins, Wythe Candy & Gourmet Shop,** or the **Peanut Shop of Williamsburg.**

WILLIAMSBURG MARKETPLACE SHOPPING

*G*eorge Washington bought earrings for his wife, Martha, at the Golden Ball. Thomas Jefferson purchased books from the Printing Office. Now you can follow in their footsteps.

Shopping with Colonial Williamsburg is an experience for the entire family. The WILLIAMSBURG Marketplace offers a wide range of shopping opportunities, varied in atmosphere and merchandise selections.

Ten shops and two outdoor sites in the Historic Area re-create the world of the colonial consumer. You'll see cocked hats, block-printed stationery, sealing wax, jewelry, baskets, Virginia hams, ceramics, and toys. If you need modern conveniences such as film and disposable cameras, just ask—they're stored discreetly under counters.

Outside the Historic Area, Colonial Williamsburg's WILLIAMSBURG brand stores carry everything from toys, logo apparel, and books in the Visitor Center stores to fine furniture and home accessories at WILLIAMSBURG At Home.

For your convenience, purchases from any Colonial Williamsburg store can be delivered to your room at one of our hotels or to the Visitor Center. In addition to cash, Colonial Williamsburg's stores accept traveler's checks and American Express, Diners Club, Discover, MasterCard, and Visa credit cards.

When you're back home, you can conveniently shop the WILLIAMSBURG Marketplace from your favorite armchair. Just call us at 1-800-446-9240 to receive our WILLIAMSBURG Marketplace catalog, or visit us online at www.WilliamsburgMarketplace.com to view our newest products. Our Web site features a wide range of merchandise, an online version of our print catalog, and convenient ways of shopping with our gift reminder and wish list services.

Whatever your shopping pleasure, whether in stores, via catalog, or online, the WILLIAMSBURG Marketplace has everything you want in one very inspiring place.

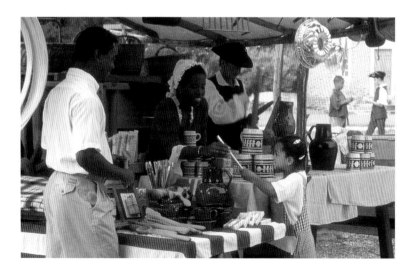

WILLIAMSBURG MARKETPLACE IN THE HISTORIC AREA

An admission ticket is not required to visit Historic Area stores.

Gateway. The Gateway building, at the end of the walking path from the Visitor Center, is a great spot to find items that will make your visit enjoyable. Here you'll find guest conveniences such as cold bottled water, sunscreen and visors, pain relievers, disposable cameras, and film, plus an assortment of well-priced gift items.

James Craig Jewelers/The Golden Ball. Guests at the Golden Ball will find many of the same jewelry pieces advertised by James Craig in the eighteenth century. Items such as reproduction stone rings, earrings, pendants, and charms in sterling silver and fourteen-karat gold are offered for sale along with the magnificent, handcrafted sterling hollowware pieces made next door at the silversmith shop. Both hand-cut and machine engraving are available on-site.

John Greenhow Store. Guests at the John Greenhow Store are amazed at the number of items listed on the eighteenth-century broadside advertisement that are still for sale in the store today. Advertised "characters" are often on hand in the store to entertain and enlighten guests to the ways of eighteenth-century mercantilism.

M. Dubois Grocer. Operating a grocer's shop on this site in the 1770s, M. Dubois advertised delicacies such as chocolate, sugar, raisins of the sun, currants, port wine, French brandy, and Seville oranges. Full of delicious smells and delectable treats for our guests of all ages, the M. Dubois Grocer is the perfect place to find favorite food gifts, such as Virginia hams or preserves.

Mary Dickinson Store. Step back in time at the Mary Dickinson Store. Handmade petticoats, short gowns, cloaks, mitts, caps, and beautifully decorated straw hats are all available for purchase. Here, mothers and their daughters will find eighteenth-century costumes and hats for dressing up in period-correct style. A wonderful assortment of jewelry and toiletries reflects eighteenth-century fashion in the best of taste.

McKenzie Shop. Today's guest in the McKenzie Shop will enjoy sampling the candies and smelling the coffee, tea, and spices, among hundreds of other items for sale in the shop.

Post Office. By the middle of 1739, the postal service in the colonies extended from Boston, Massachusetts, through principal towns in New York, Pennsylvania, Maryland, Virginia, and North Carolina and into Charleston, South Carolina. The Post Office features a large selection of color prints and reproduction printed material. Many of the forms and other printed materials are hand-set and printed "below stairs" on an eighteenth-century press. Leather-bound books, stationery, quill pens, ink, inkwells, and sealing wax are available. Guests can buy stamps as well as mail their letters and postcards, complete with a hand-canceled Williamsburg postmark.

Prentis Store. The building stands today as the best-surviving example of a colonial-period store. In continuous use as everything from an apothecary shop to an early-twentieth-century automobile service station, the basic format of the store has changed little in its 260-year history. Today, the Prentis Store offers fine-quality, handcrafted items made in the Historic Trades shops in Colonial Williamsburg's Historic Area using authentic eighteenth-century tools and methods.

Raleigh Tavern Bakery. Here you will find cookies, cakes, and breads made fresh daily from eighteenth-century recipes. Also, apple cider, root beer, and food-related gifts are available.

Tarpley's Store. As a young man, James Tarpley was apprenticed to a merchant to learn his trade and began his own store at this location in 1755. Tarpley's was not always operated as a "store" but over time served as a place of business for a jeweler, a clockmaker, and a printer. Much of the merchandise found in Tarpley's Store today is geared toward children, with colorful toys, games, candies, period clothing, hats, and jewelry.

Tickets, Treasures, and Books. This store offers many publications, games, and guest service items. A ticket office at this location has admission tickets to all Historic Area buildings, carriage rides, and evening programs. The staff welcomes guests' questions regarding their visit to historic sites, availability of tickets for special programs, and the making of dining reservations.

OPEN SEASONALLY IN THE HISTORIC AREA

Colonial Garden and Nursery. The Colonial Garden and Nursery offers a wide variety of heirloom seeds and plants for sale to our guests. Along with herbs, flowers, seasonal greens, and wreaths, our guests may also purchase period-appropriate eighteenth-century clay flowerpots and bird bottles. Children will enjoy learning

about eighteenth-century gardening as they help our trained garden historians and staff cultivate and water the plants in the colonial garden.

Market Square. Market Square is an open-air market area, with booths resembling those of the eighteenth century, selling baked goods and refreshments, as well as toys, hats, pottery, and baskets. Auctions of new goods from the Historic Area stores are scheduled weekly throughout the year. Young ladies and gentlemen are encouraged to "dress up" in the eighteenth-century costumes available to rent and to experience a taste of eighteenth-century childhood trying their skills at the hoop and stick or bilbo catcher.

CHECKLIST: SHOPPING MADE EASY

Colonial Williamsburg's stores accept the following forms of payment

☐ *Cash.*

☐ *Traveler's checks.*

☐ *American Express.*

☐ *Diners Club.*

☐ *Discover.*

☐ *MasterCard.*

☐ *Visa.*

For your convenience, purchases from any Colonial Williamsburg store can be delivered to your Colonial Williamsburg hotel or to the Visitor Center.

Call 1-800-770-5938 to order WILLIAMSBURG merchandise from home. You can also browse the WILLIAMSBURG catalog at www.WilliamsburgMarketplace.com.

WILLIAMSBURG MARKETPLACE OUTSIDE THE HISTORIC AREA

WILLIAMSBURG At Home. Don't miss our flagship store, WILLIAMSBURG At Home, located in Merchants Square. This destination offers the ultimate shopping experience for home furnishings and accessories, featuring the full line of WILLIAMSBURG furniture, bedding, rugs, lighting fixtures, prints, fabrics, and wallpapers inspired by the eighteenth century. Be sure to visit our full-service Design Studio in the store. In styles ranging from traditional to contemporary, our designers offer personal client consultation, full- or partial-room design, custom window treatments, and more. Or, relax and browse on your own through our presentation books, swatches, and in-store kiosks featuring our bedding and furniture selections and the work of our talented design staff.

WILLIAMSBURG Craft House. Regular guests of Colonial Williamsburg call this "the most important" stop of their shopping excursion. High-quality gifts and decorative accessories await—as well as one of the best selections of jewelry and ceramics in town. There is something to delight everyone within this two-level Williamsburg icon.

WILLIAMSBURG Celebrations. Experience your favorite seasons year-round, from the sights and sounds of a Williamsburg Christmas to the fragrance of a fresh spring garden. See a full assortment of holiday decorations, seasonal floral arrangements, and garden accessories galore. And don't forget to shop here for all your favorite WILLIAMSBURG collectibles.

Everything WILLIAMSBURG. Any other souvenir shop pales in comparison. Apparel for kids and adults plus our best selection of signature children's toys and souvenir gift items are all here.

Golden Horseshoe Golf Club—Gold Course Pro Shop. Celebrating forty years, this tasteful space offers the golfer and style-conscious buyer a wide selection of the top golf brand apparel for ladies and men, pl Golden Horseshoe logo merchandise. H you will find great gifts for the avid golfer from one of the top 100 golf courses in the country.

Golden Horseshoe Golf Club—Green Course Pro Shop. This shop, which overlooks the eighteenth hole, offers the golfer those must-have items such as towels, golf balls, golf gloves, and accessories. A selection of ladies' and men's logo apparel makes this a necessary stop for the fashion-conscious golfer.

WILLIAMSBURG Booksellers and **Commonwealth Coffee and Tea.** As your best resource for publications about the eighteenth century, browse hundreds of titles for adults and kids. WILLIAMSBURG Booksellers also features music CDs, videos, DVDs, and gifts for book lovers and patriots. You can enjoy gourmet coffees and teas, lattes, cappuccinos, soft drinks, and delectable pastries from the café while you browse the store, located at the Visitor Center.

WILLIAMSBURG Revolutions. Enhance your visit with a gift from WILLIAMSBURG Revolutions, a twenty-first-century shopping experience with an eighteenth-century perspective. Conveniently located at the Visitor Center, you will find gifts, toys, logo apparel, collectibles, and more. It's the perfect way to start (don't forget costume rentals) or end your day!

Regency Shop at the Williamsburg Inn. The shop reflects the history and tradition of this grand hotel, offering unique, quality gifts reminiscent of southern lifestyles and the romance of the setting. While the Inn offers the best location for anniversaries and honeymoons, the Regency Shop offers the best accompanying gifts for the occasion.

Gift Shop at the Williamsburg Lodge. A wonderful shop featuring food and gifts made in Virginia plus folk art decorative accents for the home, basic sundries, and souvenirs.

Museum Store. Surprise! This is the best-kept secret of all the Colonial Williamsburg shops. Tell the person at the reception desk that you're "just shopping" and venture downstairs to gifts and accessories reflecting current museum and institute programs.

Williamsburg Woodlands Hotel & Suites Gift Shop. Conveniently located, the gift shop features gifts, apparel, and souvenirs—plus sundries and convenience items for guests.

Promenade Kiosk at the Visitor Center. A quick and convenient stop just over the pedestrian bridge, the kiosk offers sundry items, including cameras, film, souvenirs, beverages, ice cream—even toys and gifts.

THE COLONIAL WILLIAMSBURG PRODUCTS PROGRAM

In the 1930s, the Colonial Williamsburg Foundation launched its landmark products program by authorizing manufacturers to produce authentic reproductions based on items in the Foundation's collections, from finds recovered by archaeological expeditions or found during the original restoration of Williamsburg.

Over the years, the Products program has grown dramatically. More than sixty licensed manufacturers now distribute thousands of WILLIAMSBURG products through our Colonial Williamsburg stores and through fine specialty stores nationwide.

In addition, the Products Division produces the WILLIAMSBURG Catalog, which is circulated nationwide to more than five million consumers each year, as well as an e-commerce Web site, www.Williamsburg Marketplace.com.

When you are visiting us, don't miss our twenty-four store locations to find everything from personal necessities and fine gifts in our hotel shops to a full line of WILLIAMSBURG-licensed home furnishings, decorative accessories, and tabletop items in our Craft House and WILLIAMSBURG At Home locations. Whether it's ginger cakes and cider at the Raleigh Tavern Bakery or Noah's arks and theorem paintings at the Museum Store, logo golf apparel and divot tools at the Golden Horseshoe Golf Club—Gold Course Pro Shop or the finest ladies' eighteenth-century fashions and millinery hats at the Mary Dickinson Store, our stores have what your heart desires. For a complete list of store locations and descriptions, see the latest "Guide to Dining and Shopping."

LODGING AND RECREATION

For convenience, southern hospitality, and things to do, you can't beat Colonial Williamsburg's hotels, ranging from the luxurious Williamsburg Inn to the economically priced Governor's Inn. Each offers an experience you can't find anywhere else and convenient package plans that make it easy to stay with us.

Convenience. Located adjacent to the Historic Area—or, in the case of the Colonial Houses, *in* the Historic Area—our Colonial Williamsburg hotels are just steps away from the programs and activities in the restored eighteenth-century capital. You'll also be close to our colonial dining taverns, our contemporary restaurants, and our eighteenth-and twenty-first-century stores. Leave the car at your hotel and walk to the Historic Area. Charge everything from meals to bike rentals to your room. Have your purchases from Colonial Williamsburg's stores delivered to your room at no charge.

Recreation and Activities. As a guest of Colonial Willliamsburg's hotels, you'll find complete resort facilities and activities. Sports enthusiasts will have plenty to do, from swimming to nature walks to golf on one of the Golden Horseshoe Golf Courses to relaxing in the spa. Our hotels also offer special themed programs throughout the year, such as weekends devoted to gourmet entertaining, wine tastings, or a behind-the-scenes look at Colonial Williamsburg.

Package Plans. Our package plans offer value and convenience. Many package plans include admission tickets to Historic Area sites, programs, and attractions. Some plans offer special tickets, tours, gifts, or meals. There are packages tailored to special interests, such as golf, and to seasonal events, such as Christmas.

For copies of Colonial Williamsburg's

Vacation Planner, annual calendar of events, and current package plan brochure, please call 1-800-HISTORY (447-8679). You can also make your lodging and dining reservations, purchase admission and evening program tickets, and reserve tee times by calling 1-800-HISTORY (447-8679). On the Internet, you can find information about Colonial Williamsburg's hotels and make reservations at www.colonialwilliamsburg.com.

Merchants Square. Adjacent to the Historic Area is Merchants Square, with more than forty stores in an elegant and lively retail village that blends architecture inspired by the eighteenth century with twenty-first-century shopping and dining. Here you'll find books, children's clothes, galleries, gift and specialty shops, home furnishings and furniture, jewelry, men's and women's apparel, restaurants, and specialty foods as well as the Kimball Theatre.

Conference and Meeting Facilities. You'll stage an unforgettable meeting with Colonial Williamsburg. Let Thomas Jefferson or Patrick Henry inspire participants, or have fifers and drummers escort attendees to a banquet. There are three conference hotels from which to choose and over 65,000 square feet of function space, with ballrooms of 12,000 and 7,000 square feet. For information on how Colonial Williamsburg can revolutionize your next meeting or conference, call 1-800-822-9127, or visit our Web site at www. colonialwilliamsburg.com/visit.

COLONIAL WILLIAMSBURG'S HOTELS

Williamsburg Inn. Abby and John D. Rockefeller Jr. were involved in every aspect of the design, construction, and furnishing of the Williamsburg Inn. They created one of the finest luxury hotels in North America. When the famed philanthropist first built the Inn in 1937, he insisted that "the most possible has been made of each room as regards comfort, convenience and charm." In 2001, Colonial Williamsburg continued to fulfill Rockefeller's original vision through the most extensive interior renovation in the Inn's history spanning the landmark's

public spaces and guest rooms, reducing the number from 100 to 62. The refurbishment dually addressed the contemporary needs of twenty-first-century travelers with enhanced services and amenities completing the meticulous restoration.

Just steps from the Historic Area, this elegantly appointed, warm, inviting, classic Virginia resort is now a national historical landmark. Guests have always regarded the Williamsburg Inn as their "second home." The Inn's architecture and ambience reflect those of fashionable nineteenth-century spas where fine dining and a tradition of exceptional hospitality were hallmarks. Employees pride themselves on the kind and courteous service they give every guest, from heads of state to vacationing families.

The Williamsburg Inn has welcomed hundreds of VIPs, including Queen Elizabeth and Prince Philip, the Emperor and Empress of Japan, President and Mrs. Jiang Zemin of China, and countless American presidents. The 1983 Summit of Industrialized Nations, hosted by President Ronald Reagan, and the 1995 NATO and Defense Ministers of America Conferences met at the Williamsburg Inn.

Guests in the main building stay in large, spacious rooms furnished with accurate reproductions and antiques of the English Regency style of the early nineteenth century. Providence Hall, nestled on the Inn grounds, affords guests accommodations in a garden setting. From the lobby to the guest rooms, the Inn exudes the quiet luxury of a Virginia country estate. Terraces overlooking the tranquil green countryside invite guests to pause for a moment of relaxation and reflection.

The Regency Room offers distinctive food and wines in an atmosphere of gracious elegance. Music accompanies evening dining and Sunday brunch (jacket and tie are required for dinner and jacket only for Sunday brunch). Commemorating the Inn's renovation is the addition of the Restoration Bar, a comfortably sophisticated spot perfect for enjoying cocktails and conversation before dining or as a nightcap. Superb in-room, private dining provides a casual alternative, and a traditional English afternoon tea is available.

Inn guests can engage in a variety of outdoor activities. The award-winning Golden Horseshoe Golf Courses and the spa and fitness center embrace the south side of the Inn. Just outside the door are swimming pools, tennis courts (both clay and hard surfaces are available), lawn bowling, croquet, nature trails, and jogging routes.

Children under the age of fifteen can play the nine-hole executive-length Spotswood Course at no charge when accompanied by a paying adult. Summer programs are offered for Inn guests ages five to twelve.

Williamsburg Lodge.

The restaurant offers all-you-can-eat buffets and a wonderful Sunday brunch. Enjoy lighter fare, cocktails, and conversation in the lobby bar.

The Golden Horseshoe Golf Courses, tennis courts (both clay and hard surfaces are available), lawn bowling, croquet, and outdoor heated swimming pools are literally steps away from the Lodge. Nature trails and jogging routes are nearby.

Children under the age of fifteen can play the nine-hole executive-length Spotswood Course at no charge when accompanied by a paying adult. Summer programs are offered for Lodge guests ages five to twelve.

From large conferences to small retreats, the Williamsburg Lodge Conference Center is the place for your gathering. Conference Center facilities can accommodate up to 1,000 people at a formal dinner or 1,300 for a general session. You'll find the perfect blend of inspiration, rest, and opportunity for reflection and recreation at the Lodge.

Williamsburg Lodge. The traditions of patriotism and gracious southern hospitality are yours as a guest of the Williamsburg Lodge, located next to the Historic Area. Memories created here last a lifetime. The main building was restored to its 1939 grandeur in late 2006. Along with new guesthouses, the Lodge offers a total of 323 guest rooms.

Relax in a ladder-backed rocking chair on a veranda overlooking a garden. Enjoy quiet conversation, a good book, or a pleasant daydream. Ward off winter's chill by claiming an armchair beside the fireplace in the Lodge's cypress-paneled lobby. Watch as flames from the wood-burning fire cast highlights on handcrafted folk art paintings and carvings inspired by the collection at the Abby Aldrich Rockefeller Folk Art Museum.

Guest rooms feature reproductions from the Abby Aldrich Rockefeller Folk Art Museum. Some rooms have private terraces and balconies overlooking landscaped lawns and gardens. In every season, you will find yourself relaxed, invigorated, and charmed by the surroundings and the hospitality of the

Williamsburg Woodlands Hotel & Suites.
A haven for families, the Williamsburg Woodlands Hotel & Suites is located in the Visitor Center complex. Combining the revolutionary experience of eighteenth-century history with the comfort and style of twenty-first-century hotel accommodations, the contemporary, three-story hotel offers guests the highest quality in moderately priced accommodations.

Featuring wood tones, vaulted ceilings, and expansive windows bathing the lobby in natural sunlight, guests of the Williamsburg Woodlands Hotel & Suites find a natural and comfortable environment. An oversized fireplace commands the lobby near the dining area for the daily continental breakfast (included in the room rate). The hotel has 204 guest rooms and 96 suites (with a minirefrigerator, microwave, and coffeemaker).

Dining options are sure to please in the Woodlands complex. Huzzah! features contemporary favorites with colonial charm all in a family-friendly atmosphere. Guests looking for a quick beverage or tea time snack will find a tempting selection at Commonwealth Coffee and Tea at the Visitor Center.

Families, couples, and business guests find the Woodlands an inviting haven after a day of sightseeing or meetings. Conference guests find it a quick stroll from the adjacent Williamsburg Woodlands Conference Center catering to groups of all sizes and needs with its 14,000 square feet of function space. Walking trails, miniature golf, a refreshing pool, and various other recreational activities are right outside the doors. Summer programs are offered for guests ages five to twelve.

Governor's Inn. Located a short walk from the Historic Area and convenient to the Visitor Center, the Governor's Inn is ideal for those looking for Colonial Williamsburg quality at economical prices. The Governor's Inn caters to families, singles, couples, and seniors who appreciate the value and convenience it offers.

The modern amenities of the spacious, comfortable guest rooms are enhanced by southern hospitality and service. Take a short walk to the Historic Area, casual and fine dining, and shopping.

Cool down in the sparkling swimming pool located at the Governor's Inn. Enjoy the daily continental breakfast (included in the room rate) in the lobby dining area. Summer programs are offered for Governor's Inn guests ages five to twelve.

Colonial Houses. Located in the heart of the Historic Area, the Colonial Houses combine unique eighteenth-century accommodations with twenty-first-century resort activities, restaurants, and shopping. Wake up to the sound of a carriage rolling by your window, then jog on Duke of Gloucester Street, play a round of golf at the Golden Horseshoe, or relax at the spa. Return to the Revolutionary era with a colonial-style meal at a historic tavern. You'll enjoy the best of the past and the present when you stay in one of the Colonial Houses.

The Colonial Houses range in size from larger taverns, such as the Brick House Tavern, to the tiny Lightfoot Laundry tucked away in a garden. Choose a small house for an intimate retreat or a larger one with up to sixteen rooms for a family getaway. Each Colonial House is furnished with period reproductions. Some have canopy beds, working fireplaces, and gardens. Each house also offers the amenities expected by today's vacationer: air conditioning, cable TV with in-room movies, room service, and more.

The Historic Area is outside your door, and the colonial dining taverns, contemporary restaurants, and shopping are just steps away.

Colonial Houses guests are welcome to use the Williamsburg Inn recreational facilities.

Children under the age of fifteen can play the nine-hole Spotswood Course at no charge when accompanied by a paying adult. Summer programs are offered for guests of the Colonial Houses ages five to twelve.

The Colonial Houses offer unique and memorable lodging for a retreat.

RECREATION

The following facilities are available to all guests of Colonial Williamsburg's hotels. Fees are required for some activities and the use of some facilities. See the previous descriptions for information on the facilities and activities each hotel offers its guests. Information is also available at our Web sites, www.colonialwilliamsburg.com and www.goldenhorseshoegolf.com.

Golden Horseshoe Golf Courses. Located just past the peaceful back lawn of the Williamsburg Inn and across the street from the Lodge, the Golden Horseshoe offers some of the finest golf in the country. Golfers can test their skills on two award-winning, eighteen-hole championship courses or on a nine-hole executive-length course.

Williamsburg's climate makes it possible to play the links here virtually year-round. A practice range, rental clubs, electric golf carts, and golf equipment are available, and a resident professional and his staff offer golf lessons. Both the Gold Course and the Green Course Clubhouses feature locker and dressing room facilities, pro shops, full-service restaurants, and lounges.

The celebrated Gold Course and Green Course have played hosts to several USGA Championships. World-famous golf course architect Robert Trent Jones Sr. called the par-71, eighteen-hole championship **Gold**

THE LEGEND OF THE GOLDEN HORSESHOE

The Legend of the Golden Horseshoe recalls the origins of Virginia history. In 1716, Governor Alexander Spotswood organized a daring expedition to explore the far reaches of the Virginia Colony. Spotswood, aware of the frontier's economic potential and bent on encouraging westward settlement, led a party of sixty-three men on the arduous journey.

Hugh Jones offered his account in 1724 of the toll taken by the rocky soil of the Piedmont and the Blue Ridge: "For this expedition they were obliged to provide a great Quantity of Horse-Shoes (Things seldom used in the lower Parts of the Country, where there are few Stones). The Governor, upon their Return, presented each of his Companions with a Golden Horse-Shoe, some of which I have seen studded with valuable Stones resembling the Heads of Nails."

The recipients became known as the "Knights of the Golden Horseshoe." Although several people in the nineteenth century claimed to have seen them, none of the small, golden horseshoes described by Jones has been found.

The Golden Horseshoe Golf Courses epitomize the tradition and mystique of Spotswood's expedition: the challenge of daring adventure, the enjoyment of a peaceful and spectacular environment, and the reward of completing an arduous test. Colonial Williamsburg invites you to become a modern Knight of the Golden Horseshoe as you test your skills on our three challenging golf courses.

Course "my finest" design, describing its location as "a natural arboretum upon which a great golf course has been built." The Gold Course has received numerous honors since it opened in 1963 and *Golf Digest* named it a "Best of the Best Design," recognizing it as one of Jones's top six designs worldwide. *Golf Magazine* has repeatedly awarded the classic course with its highly coveted Gold Medal. *Southern Links* named the par-3 holes the "Best of the South." The Gold Course was renovated under the supervision of Robert Trent Jones's son, Rees, who is also the architect of the Golden Horseshoe Green Course. Jack Nicklaus holds the course record of a four-under-par 67, a record that has stood since September 19, 1967.

The **Green Course** debuted in 1991 and has been repeatedly awarded "four and a half stars" by *Golf Digest's Places to Play*.

The course features abundant woodland and natural terrain that accommodates various playing skills. Course designer Rees Jones termed it "a shotmaker's course," explaining, "We did not try to make the course tell the player what to do. Instead, we tried to give him several options and allow him to hit several strokes."

Robert Trent Jones Sr. designed the par-31, nine-hole executive-length **Spotswood Course**. Players can hone their short game on this tight, demanding course, which was named the "best 9-hole short course in the country" by *Golf Magazine*. Respecting the tradition of the game, players are requested to wear regulation shoes and attire on and around the courses.

Nature and Fitness Trails. Trails are located near the Williamsburg Inn and on the grounds of the Williamsburg Woodlands

Hotel & Suites. The Historic Area is also ideal for jogging, power walking, bicycling, or leisurely strolls.

Tennis. Two all-weather and six Har-Tru® clay courts are located adjacent to the Williamsburg Inn Providence Hall. A tennis pro is available for private and semiprivate lessons. The Inn courts also feature a tennis shop where you can rent equipment, purchase tennis clothing and accessories, and register on the guest play list to find a partner. Players are requested to wear regulation tennis shoes and attire on and around the courts.

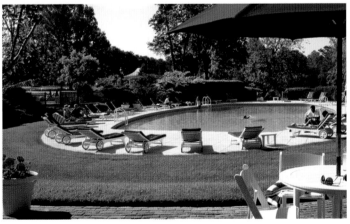

EDUCATIONAL SERVICES

As part of our mission to teach the founding idea of America, the Colonial Williamsburg Foundation offers many educational services.

Education for Citizenship. The Colonial Williamsburg Foundation believes that history should be at the very core of education. Understanding our rich American history and heritage prepares citizens to participate in the democratic process—a process that sustains the ideals of freedom and equality immortalized by our founding generation. The Colonial Williamsburg Foundation works actively to engage teachers and students in the Historic Area, in on-site workshops, and through distance learning programs across the country with our American history and the role of individual citizens in shaping our nation.

Learning Resource Center. At the Learning Resource Center, located at WILLIAMSBURG Booksellers in the Visitor Center, educators, parents, and other interested guests can examine the educational materials, programs, and opportunities for professional development offered by Colonial Williamsburg. The programs and materials here help parents and educators teach early American history. Classroom-related materials on eighteenth-century topics, including lesson plans, videos, children's literature, resource kits, and reproduction documents, are available for purchase.

Study Visits. Study visits provide students—from preschool through college—with an overview of daily life before the American Revolution. Through tours, role playing, and observing and participating in activities, students learn about the lives and choices of the men, women, and children—both free and enslaved—who inhabited the capital city of the largest British colony in North America. Call 1-800-228-8878 for information or to make reservations for study visits.

Teaching Resources. Teachers and parents can find the latest American history instructional materials on the Internet at www. history.org/teach. Offerings include Electronic Field Trips, videos, books, lesson units, Hands-on-History kits, and the free monthly *Teacher Gazette* e-newsletter. For a catalog or more information, call 1-800-761-8331.

Electronic Field Trips. Twenty-first-century communication technologies bring the excitement of American history to students across the country. Electronic Field Trips are available to educators as live interactive television events or as on-demand opportunities. Registered schools interact with Colonial Williamsburg's interpreters and use the resource-rich Web site to provide high-quality online experiences for students with e-mail, discussion forums, interactive lessons, and streaming video. To learn more about Colonial Williamsburg's Electronic Field Trip season, visit www.history.org/teach or call 1-800-761-8331.

Scouting Programs. Specialized programming for Boy Scouts and Girl Scouts is available. Call 1-800-228-8878 to find out more information.

Teacher Institute. The Colonial Williamsburg Teacher Institute is a national on-site professional development program for K–12 educators. The weeklong program is a hands-on, comprehensive experience designed to excite and inspire teachers with the legacy of our American history. Teachers immerse themselves in early American history in Colonial Williamsburg's 301-acre living history museum and trips to nearby Jamestown and Yorktown. Teachers learn how to engage their students with primary sources, history simulations, and events to make American history exciting.

Colonial Williamsburg also offers a series of one- and two-day teacher professional development workshops and programs at sites around the country. For more information, visit www.history.org/teach or call 1-800-688-6473.

Colonial Williamsburg's Web Site. Visit our Web site, www.history.org (or www.colonialwilliamsburg.org), to find a wealth of information about eighteenth-century Williamsburg, the people who lived here, and the places they inhabited. The site also contains material especially for educators, including an overview of Colonial Williamsburg's educational resources and information on Electronic Field Trips for the current school year.

John D. Rockefeller, Jr. Library. Through its specialized collections of books, journals, manuscripts, architectural drawings, and photographs, as well as a full range of on-line services, the John D. Rockefeller, Jr. Library supports and encourages research on seventeenth- and eighteenth-century colonial British America, the Revolutionary era, the early Republic, the colonial Chesapeake, African American studies, the decorative arts and material culture through 1830, archaeology, architectural history, and historical preservation. The library serves scholars, advanced students, the Foundation's staff, and the public and is open weekdays from 9:00 a.m. to 5:00 p.m.

GIFTS, BEQUESTS, AND MAJOR BENEFACTORS

*A*lthough admission tickets purchased by guests provide one major source of funds needed to support Colonial Williamsburg's educational and museum programs, the Foundation needs and encourages gifts and bequests from all who believe in our mission "that the future may learn from the past." Friends interested in discussing gifts to Colonial Williamsburg are encouraged to write to the Director of Development, The Colonial Williamsburg Foundation, P.O. Box 1776, Williamsburg, VA 23187-1776 or e-mail to gifts@cwf.org.

The Colonial Williamsburg Foundation Board of Trustees expresses its deepest thanks to *all* our donors. Since 1926, Colonial Williamsburg's honor roll of donors has grown from its original benefactors to more than 115,000 a year. Listed are Colonial Williamsburg's most generous benefactors: individuals, foundations, and corporations that have made gifts and grants of $1 million or more.

Colonial Williamsburg's Founders
John D. Rockefeller Jr. and Abby Aldrich Rockefeller

Gifts and Grants of $20 Million or More
Lila and DeWitt Wallace
DeWitt Wallace Endowment Fund
The Annenberg Foundation
June S. and Joseph H. Hennage
William R. and Gretchen B. Kimball

Gifts and Grants of $10 Million or More
City of Williamsburg
Ann Lee S. and Charles L. Brown

Gifts and Grants of $5 Million or More
Martha Baird Rockefeller
John D. Rockefeller 3rd Fund
The Winthrop Rockefeller Charitable Trust
Abby and George O'Neill
Henry H. and "Jimmy" deH. Weldon
Royce R. and Kathryn McCormick Baker
Bob and Marion Wilson
Ruth P. and Joseph R. Lasser
David and Peggy Rockefeller

Gifts and Grants of $1 Million or More

Blanchette and John D. Rockefeller 3rd
Elizabeth and Miodrag Blagojevich
Rockefeller Brothers Fund
National Endowment for the Humanities
The Kresge Foundation
The Pew Charitable Trusts
Dr. Lowry Kirby
Frances M. McDermott
Institute of Museum and Library Services
Mary Lou and George B. Beitzel
Jane and Marshall Steel Jr.
The Marshall Steel, Sr. Foundation
Ambassador Bill and Jean Lane
Pauline and Samuel M. Clarke
Louise Coon
Inez R. and C. O. Middlekauf
Letitia and Edward C. Joullian III
Mrs. T. Richard Crocker
Ambassador Randall L. and Marianne W. Tobias
Gladys M. Whitehead
Estelle and Harold Tanner
Pat and Jerry B. Epstein
Frances B. Crandol
Virginia S. and Robert L. deCourcy
Marcia and John R. Donnell Jr.
John A. Hyman and Betty C. Leviner
Marilyn L. Brown and Douglas N. Morton

Carolyn W. and James R. Millar
Shirley H. and Richard D. Roberts
Joshua P. and Elizabeth D. Darden
Leslie Anne Miller and Richard B. Worley
AT&T Foundation
IBM Corporation
Maureen M. and James W. Gorman Sr.
Virginialee and Edward Lynch
Muriel and Foster McCarl Jr.
Elizabeth M. and Joseph M. Handley
Jeanne C. and Willard O. Hoffmire
Martha A. Healy
Frank and Jane P. Batten
The Grainger Foundation
Steven and Sheila Miller Foundation
Margaret Lee and T. Marshall Hahn Jr.
Sally B. and Theodore W. Brickman Jr.
Alma Louise and Harry H. Coon
Paul F. Miller Jr. and Ella Warren Miller
Alan B. and Janet M. Coleman
Penelope P. and Dr. Sergio V. Proserpi
Lilly Endowment Inc.
Lois and Dick Vieser
The Gladys and Franklin Clark Foundation
Nancy N. and Colin G. Campbell
Alice C. and Richard G. Tilghman
John and Linda Muckel

**Special thanks to the Steven and Sheila Miller Foundation
for support of this guidebook.**

INDEX

Boldface page numbers indicate illustrations. An asterisk indicates that a building is an original eighteenth- or nineteenth-century structure. A blue box indicates that you need an admission ticket to see an attraction.

Americans at, 82, 101; bell at, 100; construction and restoration of, 100, 123; establishment of, 94, 99–100; first, 99–100; funding for, 64, 100, 101, 128; graves surrounding, 100–101; and growth of Williamsburg, 19; importance of, 32, 99; members of, 31, 44, 64, 80, 100, 125; naming of, 99; Pelham as organist for, 74; pictures of, **32**, **100**; rectors of, 132; and restoration of Williamsburg, 24; second, 100; services at, 101; sightseeing at, 32; and town plan, 17; tradesmen near, 96; vestry for, 99, 100, 101, 125. *See also* Anglican church; Church of England

Bryan House, 103, **103**
Bryan, William, 103
Bucktrout, Benjamin, 118, 129
Burnaby, Andrew, 15
Burwell, John, 123
Burwell, Lewis, 59
Burwell, Sally (Mrs. John Bracken), 132
buses. *See* shuttle buses
Byrd, William, II (of Westover), 88–89

cabinetmaker. *See* Hay's Cabinet-making Shop
Caesar (slave), 115
Campbell, Christiana, 124
Campbell, Christiana, Tavern. *See* Christiana Campbell's Tavern
■Capitol,12; activities at, 67–68; during American Revolution, 21, 23; and Bodleian Plate, **17**, 24; construction/reconstruction of, 24, **68**, 108, 123; courts in, 45, 69–70; design of, 68, **68**, 69; dining and shopping near, 28; doorkeepers at, 75; fire at, 69, 72, 108; first, 67, 69; flags on, **69**; floor plan of, **68**; furnishings in, 70; General Assembly in, 67–69, 70; grammar school in, 127; and growth of Williamsburg, 18, 19; keeper of keys to, 123; modern legislature meetings in, **76**; offices in, 70; pictures of, **67**, **68**; second, 67, 69; sightseeing around the, 29–31; sightseeing from Market Square to the, 50–61; and town plan, 16, 17; and Virginians declaring independence from England, 70, 72
Carlos, Elizabeth, 123–24
Carlos, Elizabeth, House. *See*

Elizabeth Carlos House
carpenters, 18, 33, 114. *See also* Elkanah Deane Shop; Great Hopes Plantation
carriage and wagon rides, 11–12, 31, 37, 159
Carter, Charles, 81
Carter, James, 58, 81
Carter, John, 58
Carter, John, Store. *See* John Carter's Store
Carter, Robert, 81
Carter, Robert, House. *See* Robert Carter House
Carter, Robert "King," 81
Carter, Robert, Kitchen. *See* Robert Carter Kitchen
Carter, Robert, Office. *See* Robert Carter Office
Catherine Blaikley House, 103, **103**
cemeteries/graveyards, 99, 100, 101, **101**
Charlton, Edward, 59
*Charlton House, 58, 59
checklist: on dining, 28, 34, 151, 153; for the first-time guest, 12; on getting to Williamsburg, 10; for home cooking, 156; on packing, 9; on planning your visit, 8; on shopping, 28, 34, 159; on staying in a Colonial Williamsburg hotel, 163; on visiting Colonial Williamsburg's Historic Area, 7
Cheese Shop, 156
children's activities, 35–39, 165, 166
Chiswell, John, 129
Chiswell-Bucktrout House, 129, **130**
Chowning, Josiah, 43, 48, 52, 152
Chowning's Tavern, 28, 35–36, 43, 48, **48**, 151, 152, **152**, 153
Christiana Campbell's Tavern, 28, 124, **124**, 133, 151, 152, **152**, 153
Christmas, 160, 162
Church of England, 32, 64, 101, 108, 127, 128. *See also* Anglican church; Bruton Parish Church
churches. *See* religion; *specific denomination or church*
"Citizens at War" (performance), 23
Civil War, 7, 14, 24, 47, 64, 109, 119
Cogar Shop, 125, **125**
Coke, John, 119, 147
Coke, John, Office. *See* John Coke Office

Coke, Robey, 119
Coke, Sarah, 119
*Coke-Garrett House, 119, **119**, 123
Cole, Jesse, 102
Cole, Roscow, 47
Cole, Roscow, House. *See* Roscow Cole House
"Collapse of the Royal Government" (performance), 23
College of William and Mary: alumni of, 32, 104, 106, 107, 127; during American Revolution, 22; "blue room" at, 108–9; and Bodleian Plate, **17**; chapel of, 108; charter for, 14, 105–6, 109; classroom at, **109**; construction of, 109; crypt at, 108; curriculum at, 106–7, 109; daily life at, 108; dining and shopping near, 28; enrollment at, 106; faculty of, 85, 107, 108–9, 127; fire at, 109; first building of, 15; Flat Hat Club at, 126; formation of, 94; great hall/dining room of, 108; and growth of Williamsburg, 18; importance of, 32, 95; Jefferson as architect for, 108; Jefferson's comments about, 107; kitchen at, 108; legislative meetings at, 69, 95, 108; Native Americans at, 106, 108, 109; in post-Revolutionary War years, 24; presidents of, 55, 103, 107, 108–9, 132; representation to House of Burgesses from, 68; setting for, 105; sightseeing around, 32; students at, 40, 47, 91, 113, 126; and theater productions, 105; and town plan, 16, 17; and Williamsburg establishments, 105. *See also* Brafferton; President's House; Wren Building
Collinson, Peter, 135
Colonial Garden and Nursery, 28, 32, 102, 159
Colonial Houses (accommodations), 162, 168, **168**
The Colonial Williamsburg Foundation, 8, 25, 48, 140, 146, 150, 161, 172, 174
Colonial Williamsburg Teacher Institute, 172–73
Commonwealth Coffee and Tea, 151, 160–61, 167
conference and meeting facilities, 163, 165, 166, 167
Constitution, U. S., 14, 31, 71, 85, 126
consumerism, 11, 17–18, 90

French and Indian War
Shields, James, 63, 153
Shields Stable, 129, 130
Shields Tavern, 28, 36, 63, **63**, 129, 151, 153
■Shoemaker's Shop, 26, 32, 97, **97**
shopping, 7, 28, 34, 157, **157**, 158–59
Shurcliff, Arthur, 148
shuttle buses, 9, 12, 27
Sign of the Rhinoceros, 54, **54**
silver/silversmiths, 17, 29, 58, 96, 119, 141, **143**, 158. *See also* The Golden Ball (silversmith)
slavery: as institution, 61. *See also* African Americans; slaves
slaves: during American Revolution, 14, 22, 23, 32–33; auctions of, 30, 43; on back streets, 111; baptism of, 82, 101; and consumer goods, 90; of Craig family, 58; and cultural sharing, 61; daily life of, 79; and Declaration of Independence, 23, 71; Dunmore offers freedom to, 14, 22, 23; of Everard family, 31, 81, 82; family life of, 49; freeing of, 24, 85; at Governor's Palace, 82, 92, 93; at Great Hopes Plantation, 39, 116; and growth of Williamsburg, 18, 19–20; importation of, 15; laws about, 61; of Moody family, 44; of Nicolson, 64; around Palace Green, 79; personal possessions of, 79; population of, 61; at the Quarter, 132; of Randolph family, 32–33, 38, 114, 115; and religion, 82, 101, 128, 131; and rise of plantation system, 61; runaway, 32–33, 73, 79, 115; Stith's bequest to, 55; trials of, 45; of Vobe, 131; of Wetherburn, 30, 59; of Wythe family, 38, 85
Small, William, 107
Smith, Israel, 147
Smith, John, 7
Smith, Robert, 136
smokehouses, 81, 84, 111, 114, 125, **148**
Southall, James, 30
Southall, James, Tavern. *See* James Southall's Tavern
special programs, 11, 31, 37, 159
Spotswood, Alexander, 16, 46, 80, 88–89, 91, 93, 100, 170
stables: on back streets, 111, 130, 132; at George Davenport House, 127; at Governor's Palace, 93; Magazine as, 18, **47**; at Peyton Randolph

House, 114; at Shields Tavern, 130; as slave quarters, 59. *See also* Ludwell-Paradise Stable; Taliaferro-Cole Stable
Stamp Act, 8, 14, 21–22, 40, 64–65
Steeps Tea Tavern & Elixir Bar, 156
Stephanos Pizza & Subs, 156
Steuben, Baron von, 53, 60, 153
Stith, Mary, 55
Stith, Mary, House. *See* Mary Stith House
Stith, William, 55
stocks. *See* pillory and stocks
Sweeney, George Wythe, 85

tailor. *See* Margaret Hunter Shop. *See also* Durfey Shop; James Moir Shop; Robert Nicolson Shop
Taliaferro, Charles, 102
Taliaferro, Elizabeth. *See* Wythe, Elizabeth Taliaferro
Taliaferro, Richard, 83, 85, 89
*Taliaferro-Cole House, 101, 102, **102**
■*Taliaferro-Cole Shop (harness-maker and saddler), 32, 102, **102**
■Taliaferro-Cole Stable (African American Religion Exhibit), 101, 102
Tarpley, James, 57, 100, 159
Tarpley's Store, 28, 56–57, **59**, 159
taverns and ordinaries: between Palace Green and College of William and Mary, 105; differences between modern and, 58–59; on Duke of Gloucester Street, 129, 130; and family activities, 35, 36; and growth of Williamsburg, 18; in Market Square area, 43; from Market Square to the Capitol, 50–51. *See also* Brick House Tavern; Chowning's Tavern; Christiana Campbell's Tavern; the Eagle Tavern; Edinburgh Castle Tavern; Hartwell Perry's Tavern; James Southall's Tavern; King's Arms Tavern; Market Square Tavern; Moody Tavern; Raleigh Tavern; Shields Tavern; Wetherburn's Tavern
taxes, 64, 101, 128
*Tayloe House, 116, **116**
Tayloe, John, 92, 116
Tayloe Kitchen, **116**
*Tayloe Office, 116, **116**
teacher institutes, 172–73
teaching resources, 172

tennis courts, 165, 166, 171
theaters, 121. *See also* Kimball Theatre; Play Booth Theater
■*Thomas Everard House, 31, 80–81, **80**, 82
Thomas Everard Office, **80**
Thomasin (slave), 44
Thompson, Mary, 92
ticket sale locations, 11, 12, 34, 105, 159, 163
tickets: for carriage and wagon rides, 11–12, 37; discount, 9–10; for evening programs, 33, 34; for guests with special needs, 9–10; and package plans, 162; as passport to sites and programs in Historic Area, 8, **9**; for special programs, 37; types of admission, 8; and use of shuttle buses, 12. *See also specific location*
Tickets, Treasures, and Books, 11, 31, 33, 34, 159
Tories. *See* loyalists
Townshend Acts, 40, 62
Travis, Edward Champion, 137
*Travis House, 137, **137**
Treaty of Paris (1783), 60–61
Trellis Restaurant and Café, 156
Tucker, St. George, 47, 80, 127, 133
Tucker, St. George, House. *See* St. George Tucker House
Tyler, John, 100, 134–35, 147

Unicorn's Horn, 58, **59**
Upshur, Abel Parker, 147

Venus (slave), 82
Vidal, John, 69–70
Virginia: charter for, 46; Declaration of Rights for, 14, 22, 104; and independence, 70, 71, 72; living conditions in, 87; map of (1755), **77**; state constitution for, 22, 104
Virginia Convention (1788), 22, 126
Virginia Gazette, 8, 51, 54, 56, 57, 60, 74, 82–83, 97, 118, 126
Visitor Center, 11, 27, 36; costume rentals at, 37; dining at, 151, 153, 167; educational resources at, 172; and guests with special needs, 9–10; hotels near, 167; and international guests, 10; restrooms at, 35; shops/kiosks at, 157, 161, 167, 172; shuttle buses at, 12; ticket sales at, 33, 34
Vobe, Jane, 53, **53**, 60, 131